MINIS TO GOD

M000282696

KEY
TO A PROSPEROUS
LIFE/CHURCH
FILLED WITH
GOD'S
POWER, MIRACLES
WONDERS &
SIGNS

LEONARD MP KAYIWA

Unless otherwise indicated, all Scripture
quotations are taken from the
New King James Version of the Bible.

original formatted and typed
by Billie Jane Hemphill
revised 2016 by John Hayward

cover design and illustrations
by Heidi Priddy
hidonia@cox.net

Ministering To God
ISBN 0-9717609-0-X
Copyright © 2002 by Leonard MP Kayiwa

All rights reserved. Written permission must be
secured from the publisher to use or reproduce
any part of this book, except for brief quotations
in critical reviews or articles.

Printed in the United States of America

Leonard Kayiwa Ministries
P.O. Box 1898
Bolingbrook, IL 60440

Dedication

This book is dedicated
to the people in
Africa, America,
Europe, China,
Australia,
Middle East, etc.,
And
To all churches
Around the world
Plus,
Those who have worked
with me to make the book available
to the Nations:
my wife Dr. Gail Kayiwa
and my children

Moses Emmanuel Kayiwa,
Joshua Israel Kayiwa,
Enoch DeoGracious Kayiwa,
and
Mary Deborah NaKayiwa

Endorsements

This book reminds me of the Words of our Lord Jesus Christ to the Pharisees in Matthew 9:11-13, "And when the Pharisees saw it, they said to His disciples. 'Why does your Teacher eat with tax collectors and sinners?"

When Jesus heard that, He said to them, "Those who are well have no need of a physician, but those who are sick. But go and learn what this means: 'I desire mercy and not sacrifice. For I did not come to call the righteous, but sinners to repentance.'"

This is not Leonard's Book; it's God's Book. On every page of this book radiates a beam of Holy light of Revelation knowledge of God by the Holy Spirit. When reading it, you just feel the Holy, awesome presence of God.

The Book speaks for itself. This is God speaking to us through this Book. Thank God Leonard obeyed and wrote it.

I don't have adequate words to say on this work of God, only thank God it is in your hands.

Apostle Carol Garver
Incorruptible Seed Ministries

This book will help people to know more about God, and help them dig deeper into the Word of God.

Bishop Lee V. Brown
Church Of God In Christ

This book opens a special dimension in the relationship between God and the individual believer as well as the corporate body of believers in any local church.

In every generation, God is looking not only for individuals but also for groups of people who will worship Him in Spirit and Truth. "Ministering to God" brings this foundational component of the Christian faith within reach of any reader who will approach it with a receptive heart, regardless of race, nationality, or religious background.

Rev. Leonard Kayiwa's obedience to the Holy Spirit in writing this book spans the gap between religion and relationship towards God and fellow human beings. In very simple and clear language, the author has delineated the fact that one cannot love God without worshipping Him; neither can one love God without loving fellow human beings.

The ultimate impact of this book on our generation will be measured by each reader's response to the practical and Scriptural basis on which Rev. Kayiwa has shared his pastoral and apostolic experiences. He has rightly divided the Word and given credit to God in every chapter of this book.

Professor Joseph B. Mukasa
B.A. (Hons. English) B.A. (High Hons. Ministry)
M. A. (Theater Arts) M.A. (Bib. Lit.)
M. Div., Ph.D. (Dramatic Arts)

Too often worship becomes another religious experience. But worship must remain an attitude towards God and His ability to be God in our lives. When worship is a lifestyle, it results in His presence making us His witnesses in the earth. Our worship is fulfilled and consummated in our daily living.

Apostle Leonard is very candid in testifying first-hand of his experience with the power and presence of God in his book.

You will know the necessity of worship, the Word of God, and the Holy Spirit being present and active in your life and the life of every believer.

I encourage you to read this "easy to read" book on ministering to God.

E.L. Warren, Presiding Prelate
International Network of Affiliate Ministries
Sr. Pastor of Cathedral of Worship
Quincy, Illinois, U.S.A.

Forward

YOU CAN DO ALL THINGS THROUGH CHRIST
WHO STRENGTHENS YOU.
THERE IS STRENGTH IN GOD AWAITING YOU.

A life/church void of God's power, miracles, wonders and signs is not what the Lord God Almighty intended. Weakness in the spirit, coupled with confusion in the mind is not at all God's vision for you and the church.

A life/church that ministers to God cannot be void of God's strength, direction and prosperity. A life/church that rightly divides the Word of God cannot lack the gifts of the Holy Spirit in manifestation. **"Those who do wickedly against the covenant he shall corrupt with flattery; but the people who know their God shall be strong, and carry out great exploits." Daniel 11:32**

Jesus, Himself, the Son of God, needed and operated in the miracles, wonders, signs, power and the anointing of God. He functioned in the Word of Knowledge, Word of Wisdom, and discernment of spirits. He was anointed. **"How God anointed Jesus of Nazareth with the Holy Spirit and with power, who went about doing good and healing all who were oppressed by the devil, for God was with Him." Acts 10:38**

And Jesus said, **"Most assuredly, I say to you, he who believes in Me, the works that I do he will do also; and greater works than these he will do, because I go to my Father."" John 14:12**

God desires to do greater works through your life/church than even Jesus did when He was here physically on earth. God shall raise the dead through your life/church — the time is NOW. Through this book, you shall be able to take your place in God with understanding.

Leonard MP Kayiwa

Bishop Leonard MP Kayiwa, D.D

About the Author

Bishop/Pastor Leonard MP Kayiwa is one of the foremost anointed men of God on earth today. His services are characterized with miracles, wonders, signs and a lot of power. Many people have been healed, delivered, saved, and filled with the Holy Spirit through his life. He is a man who loves Jesus Christ, loves the Holy Spirit and loves God, the Father.

Through the call of an apostle on his life, he has stood with many churches to bring them to a realm of strength in God. Leonard is author of three other books:

1) **What Happens When We Pray and Believe God;**
2) **Receive Your Healing in The Name of Jesus Christ of Nazareth;**
3) **You Can Prosper In God.**

God called Leonard Kayiwa from a background of engineering. He went to Makerere University, Uganda, East Africa and Hahai University, Nanjing, China. He came from a Catholic Church background. But he got born again in 1981 Uganda and filled with the Holy Spirit with evidence of speaking in tongues in 1985 at Kowloon Island, Hong Kong, China. He is a Ugandan by birth and was ordained in a full gospel church.

He is a student of the Bible. He did his Bible training with ICBI, based in Brussels, Belgium. He now preaches and teaches holding crusades around the world. Has a doctorate in Divinity.

God does unusual miracles by his hands. Even by aprons taken from his body to the sick, the diseases and evil spirits leave the people.

He has appeared on television in Uganda and on the radio in the U.S.A..

God has used him to help many people who are called to stand in the offices of apostle, prophet, evangelist, pastor, and teacher, to go forth in their destiny - a blessing to the Body of Christ.

"I watched
till thrones were put
in place,
and the ancient of days
was seated;
his garment was white as
snow, and the hair of his
head was like
pure wool.
His throne was a fiery
flame, its wheels
a burning fire;
a fiery stream issued
and came forth from
before him.
a thousand thousands
ministered to him;
ten thousand times
ten thousand
stood before him.
The court was seated,
and the books were opened."
Daniel 7:9-10

Table of Contents

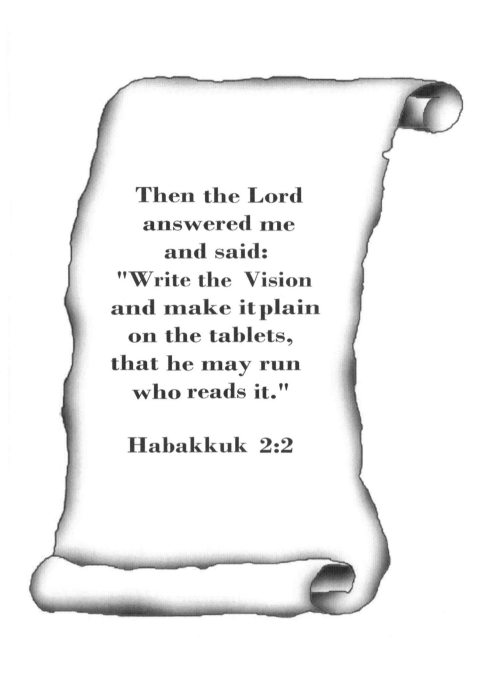

Then the Lord
answered me
and said:
"Write the Vision
and make it plain
on the tablets,
that he may run
who reads it."

Habakkuk 2:2

MINISTERING

TO

GOD

Key to Overcoming
Territorial Evil Spirits

"...Or how can one enter
a strong man's house
and plunder his goods, unless he
first binds the strong man?
And then he will plunder his house."
Matthew 12:29

In 1989, the Lord spoke to me to go and start a church on the eastern side of Kampala. Kampala is the capital city of Uganda, and Uganda is in East Africa. This place seemed to be different from all the other areas in the city. People were getting born again and getting filled with the Holy Spirit in the western side of Kampala, as well as the northern side of the city. For this territory on the eastern side, called "Kamwokya," nothing was happening. Even the Pentecostal, or Bible believing churches in that area, instead of increasing in the power of God, as well as in numbers were just dwindling and some had to shut down. It seemed as if, when the devil was conquered in the other territories, he just went to the eastern side of the city and took it over.

And these were times of great visitation in the other areas of the city! People were getting delivered. Churches were increasing in numbers and miracles, wonders and signs were taking place every day. But with Kamwokya and surrounding areas, it was as if dead. The sad thing about it, the eastern side of Kampala had a lot of people living there.

When God spoke to me to go and begin a church there, I was still co-pastoring a church in Ggaba, a Full-Gospel Church. During those days, because of the Apostolic call on my life — that is a call to stand in the office of an apostle — a number of pastors around the city of Kampala used to invite me to minister in their churches - the gift God has put in your life will always make room for you. **"A man's gift makes room for him, and brings him before great men."** Proverbs 18:16 You know the five-fold ministry is a must for the body of Christ. **"And He Himself gave some to be apostles, some prophets, some evangelists, and some pastors and teachers, for the equipping of the Saints for the work of ministry, for the edifying of the Body of Christ...."** Ephesians 4:11-13 In this light of the Word, it's clear that all these offices are available to the Body of Christ and the world at large today. Fortunately, some of the pastors understood the need of the other offices for the building of saints.

God enabled me to be part of the great move in Uganda at that time. I did know and see the difference the eastern side of Kampala had from the rest of the other areas. In that area, there were many Moslems and there were also other traditional religious churches who never knew that someone had to get born again.

It was also an area where nearly one-tenth of the population was involved in brewing beer and drinking heavily. There were a number of witch doctors, sorcerers, and magicians as well.

The proper description of the situation was like that of **Acts 8:9-11. "But there was a certain man called Simon, who previously practiced sorcery in the city and astonished the people of Samaria claiming that he was someone great, to whom they all gave heed, from the least to the greatest saying, 'This man is the**

great power of God, and they heeded him because he had astonished them with his sorceries for a long time.'"

People in Kamwokya had been astonished with all kinds of destructive beliefs and styles of life. They did not know the power of God. They were as if shut off from the blessings of the Lord God Almighty.

The resistance in the atmosphere was very strong. This area was adamant to the move of God. There was a principality over this area — that is, an evil power, like that which was described in the book of Daniel — that prince of the air that resisted the messenger angel sent to Daniel by God.

"Then he said to me, 'Do not fear, Daniel, for from the first day that you set your heart to understand, and to humble yourself before your God, your words were heard; and I have come because of your words. But the Prince of the Kingdom of Persia withstood me twenty-one days; and behold, Michael, one of the chief princes, came to help me, for I had been left alone there with the King of Persia.'" Daniel 10:12-13

Their desire is for the plan of Satan to be established on people's lives instead of God's plan as He says in **Jeremiah 29:11-12, "For I know the thoughts that I think toward you, says the Lord, thoughts of peace and not of evil, to give you a future and a hope. Then you will call upon Me and go and pray to Me, and I will listen to you."**

Our Lord Jesus Christ pointed out in Matthew 12:29 that to take over these territories, or to plunder their houses or the areas they hold captive, they have to be disarmed, bound, and their powers over the people have to be destroyed. **"Or how can one enter a strong man's house and plunder his goods, unless he first binds the strong man? And then he will plunder his house." Matthew 12:29**

Remember, the Lord had just healed a man who was demon-possessed, blind and mute. The word, "demon-possessed," literally means that he was a possession of demons. The devils had him as one of their "goods" which our Lord brought to an end by casting out the devils and freeing the man.

THE LORD GIVES ME THE STRATEGY OF FREEING THAT AREA — MINISTERING TO GOD

The Lord spoke to me to go to Kamwokya and start His church among the people, right in that place. The Lord told me that I needed to teach them, as well as gather the people who are willing to start ministering to God within that area. He said to me, *"Gather My people to worship Me."*

The Lord explained to me that in every service we needed to take time to ascribe glory and honor and power to Him, respective of the circumstances. That is exactly what I did. I started with one person joining me the first time I began services. I named the church "Christian Faith Center" as the Lord directed.

The Bible says in **John 10:4, "And when he brings out his own sheep, he goes before them; and the sheep follow him, for they know his voice."** You and I, we know the voice of the Lord, so I knew Him when He spoke. The Lord told me that as we concentrate on ministering to Him, He will manifest His Glory in our midst. Demons, plus the territorial evil principality that had been holding that area would be broken. That is exactly what I did. We began every service in this kind of flow:

"You are worthy, Lord God, thou who made the heavens and earth. As Your Word says, **'In the beginning God created the heavens and the earth.' Genesis 1:1** The earth is thine, Lord, and all its fullness, the world and those who dwell therein, **'The earth is the Lord's, and all its fullness, the World and those who dwell therein.' Psalms 24:1** Kamwokya, Eastern Kampala, is yours and all its fullness and all those who dwell therein.

Though in the natural it looked different, we just stayed with the fact of what the Word of God says God is and what He says is His. (When you do that, you are ministering to the Lord. Ministering to the Lord is so much about ascribing greatness to God and acknowledging plus declaring, as well as establishing the fact that He is the Lord God, with absolute power.)

You are Almighty God. **"When Abram was ninety-nine years old, the Lord appeared to Abram and said to him, 'I am Almighty God; walk before me and be blameless. And I will make my covenant between me and you, and will multiply you exceedingly.'" Genesis 17:1-2**

As you notice in this Bible Scripture, what I have done is to ascribe to Him what He has revealed Himself to be by declaring it in the Heavens and on the Earth. This is exactly what we did in Kamwokya. All the atmosphere started changing as the Glory of the Lord filled the place. I mean a tangible presence of God that could be felt. It was as if the area was electrified the more we said, *"All power belongs to you and there is nothing too hard for you,"* the more the presence of God filled the area. The Word of God says in **Jeremiah 32:27, "Behold, I am the Lord, the God of all flesh. Is there anything too hard for me?"** I would like to call to your attention the fact that when you are ministering to God, your attention or focus is on Him.

Your wording is centered on Him, not you, neither about the problem, nor about the devils, and not about other people.

For example, in the Book of II Chronicles, when a big army came against Jehoshaphat and the children of Israel, there was such a great multitude they did not in the natural have power against that army. **"O our God, will you not judge them? For we have no power against this great multitude that is coming against us, nor do we know what to do, but our eyes are upon you." II Chronicles 20:12** In fact, they did not know what to do. It was as if this invading army had seized the territory and brought in a hopeless situation.

In Jehoshaphat's prayer to the Lord God Almighty concerning this situation, we see him ministering to God. He verbally ascribed power to Him and affected the outcome of the event. He dealt with it from the point of God's strength.

"Then Jehoshaphat stood in the assembly of Judah and Jerusalem, in the house of the Lord, before the new court, and said: 'Lord God of our Fathers, are you not God in Heaven, and do you not rule over all the kingdoms of the nations, and in your hand is there not power and might, so that no one is able to withstand you?'" II Chronicles 20:5-12

If you look at the proclamation/prayer of Jehoshaphat you will notice he was talking to God directly and glorifying Him irrespective of the circumstances. He ascribed all the power to Him.

The Bible says, in **Proverbs 3:5, "Trust in the Lord with all your heart, and lean not on your own understanding; in all your ways acknowledge Him, and He shall direct your paths."** This is what Jehoshaphat did: he blessed the Lord. **"Bless the Lord, O my soul, and all that is within me, bless His Holy Name!" Psalms 103:1**

In his prayer, he ministered to God. His praying is not problem-centered, it is God-centered. He proclaimed and declared in the heavens that the Lord had absolute power even in that situation. This blessed God. This is what happens when people in a church or as individuals minister to God. To God it is like a sweet, soothing aroma. **"Then Noah built an altar to the Lord, and took of every clean animal and of every clean bird, and offered burnt offerings on the altar. And the Lord smelled a soothing aroma. Then the Lord said in His heart...." Genesis 8:20-22**

Through ministering to God, you bless him. You please Him; you ultimately touch God's heart. Jehoshaphat's prayer must have been like a soothing aroma to God. No wonder God responded so strongly to Jehoshaphat's prayer and brought about the solution and the strategy to defeat the enemies of Judah.

"Then the Spirit of the Lord came upon Jahaziel the son of Zechariah, the son of Benaiah, the son of Jeiel.......in the midst of the assembly and He said, listen all you of Judah, and you inhabitants of Jerusalem, and you King Jehoshaphat! Thus says the Lord to you: 'Do not be afraid nor dismayed because of this great multitude, for the battle is not yours, but God's.......You will not need to fight in this battle. Position yourselves, stand still and see the salvation of the Lord who is with you, O Judah and Jerusalem.' Do not fear or be dismayed. Tomorrow go out against them, for the Lord is with you." II Chronicles 20:14-17

That is God speaking back to His people and what happened after was amazing. The Bible says God set ambushes against this army. "Now when they began to sing and to praise, the Lord sent ambushes against the people of Ammon, Moab, and Mount Seir, who had come against Judah; and they were defeated. For the people of Ammon and Moab stood up against the inhabitants of Mount Seir to utterly kill and destroy them. And when they had made an end of the inhabitants in Seir, they helped to destroy one another."
II Chronicles 20:22-23.

This army was definitely motivated by Satan and the demons working with him. His intention was to take over that territory, to kill, destroy and enslave the people of God. Though, in the natural, you could see people invading, in the invisible realm the wicked one was working with them.

The Book of Job portrays a similar picture. **"And a messenger came to Job and said, 'The oxen were plowing and the donkeys feeding beside them, when the Sabeans raided them and took them away — indeed they have killed the servants with the edge of the sword; and I alone have escaped to tell you!'" Job 1:14-15**

It is very clear in the Book of Job, the first chapter, twelfth verse, that the devil was the driving force behind all the disasters that came on Job.

TERRITORIAL EVIL SPIRITS DISARMED THROUGH MINISTERING TO GOD IN KAMWOKYA

As you will recall, I began the first service in Kamwokya with one person attending, in a small place that could accommodate something like thirty people. The first day we ministered to God, saying, *"Lord, your power destroys all the powers of the enemy, and no stronghold can withstand your presence. Wisdom belongs to you, and sound counsel in Jesus Christ is yours!"*

The power of God hit the place! The place got electrified. The people, in the surrounding area of the place of worship, started feeling the change in the atmosphere because of the increasing magnitude of the tangible presence of the God as we took time to minister to Him, speaking out to the Lord.

People started coming forth to worship the Lord. Within one month, the place was so full that I needed more space. It was clear that God's power was destroying the demons and the powers of satan in that area.

People could come and join the services. Every day people were getting born again, healed and set free, filled with the Holy Spirit, with evidence of speaking in tongues. People started coming in for prayer and counseling.

In this area were some people who never knew that Jesus was the Son of God. In their Islam religion, they had been told that God could not have a son. But they were attracted to our services for God's presence was real among us and God was supplying people's needs according to His riches in Glory by Christ Jesus.

"And my God shall supply all your need according to His riches in Glory by Christ Jesus." Philippians 4:19

A Moslem lady came to one of our services at the invitation of her neighbor. She was experiencing severe back problems and she felt like something was moving down her legs and up to her neck, a number of times in her body. She had lived with this infirmity for ten years. The doctors had identified it as a severe blood disorder, and those at the Mosque where she attended prayers, the Imams, could not help her. There was no remedy for her suffering in the religion of Islam she belonged to and had attended all her life. She was around 55 years old.

On hearing about the wonderful testimonies the Lord God was performing in our midst in the Name of Jesus Christ, the Son of God, she stepped out for prayer. I could see that God was already delivering her from Satan's bondage, for the power of God was tangibly working in her life causing the devils that had oppressed her all that time to manifest.

You, who are reading this book, need to understand that there are demons out there, that is why in Mark 16:17, Jesus said, **"and these signs will follow those who believe, in my name, they will cast out demons...."** When the power of God is present and flowing in a service, demons can't hide any more. This power burns them like fire, as in this lady's case, what the doctors and other physicians and religious leaders thought was just a physical illness, it was worse than that. When I began to pray for her, the unclean spirits started crying out saying that there was fire from God destroying them. They cried out so loudly and came out of this Moslem woman convulsing greatly and within ten minutes she was completely delivered. She checked her back and there was no more pain. The bad presence in her body was gone. She was full of joy and she praised the Lord God Almighty and asked what she should do to get born again, as it happened in Acts 16:20-21. **"And he brought them out and said, "Sirs, what must I do to get saved." So they said, "Believe in the Lord Jesus Christ and you will be saved, you and your household."** Well, we led her into the Prayer of Salvation, she got born again that exact moment, and also was filled with the Holy Spirit with evidence of speaking in tongues, for the Lord Jesus Christ baptized her with the Holy Spirit and Fire (Luke 3:16) **"John answered, saying to all, 'I indeed baptize you with water; but one mightier than I is coming whose sandal string I am not worthy to loose, He will baptize you with the Holy Spirit and Fire."** This is exactly what happened to that precious lady who became a Christian that day. Later, she brought her children as well as her husband, the whole family came, and we baptized them in Lake Victoria in Kampala, Uganda. It was such a very glorious moment, the whole family embraced Jesus Christ as their personal Savior, and they all were baptized in the Holy Spirit, with evidence of speaking in tongues. In addition, those devils which had tormented them for a long time were totally crushed. This family lived and enjoyed their new experience in Christ Jesus and attended services nearly every day.

Beloved, ministering to God is a must for our individual lives as well as a must to accomplish our divine mission of winning the lost for the Kingdom of God, for the Gospel must come to people, not in word only but also in power. **"For our gospel did not come to you in word only, but also in power, and in The Holy Spirit and in much assurance, as you know what kind of men we were among you for your sake."** I **Thessalonians 1:5**

Ministering to God puts us in a position to receive divine intervention from God. We took back the eastern side of Kampala through the power of God. The enemy was dethroned.

News went around that God was mightily using a young man of twenty-seven years, with other believers and mighty things were happening, like the healing of tumors in the name of Jesus Christ, casting out demons in the name of Jesus Christ, breaking spells over peoples' lives, barren wombs being opened. People were being healed of cancer, AIDS, mental problems. People were set free from all kinds of addictions - like alcohol, smoking, and prostitution.

People from Islam and other of traditional churches started getting born again and receiving Christ as their personal Saviour for the first time.

The place was ablaze with heavenly fire. Yokes were being broken and burdens were being removed off people because of the anointing. Blinders were being removed so they could see and exercise their will.

We had to pull down the back wall and enlarge our service place. Most of the people in Kamwokya were busy talking about Jesus and the power of God, for they had never seen the presence of God manifested to that extent in the church services they attended. They did not know that in the Name of Jesus Christ, God still heals, gives jobs, gives wisdom, speaks and reveals conditions about their challenges, and frees, as well as helps people today as it happened then in the Bible days.

The point I want to make here is that this level of operation is available to every believer and church around the world. This did not happen because God loves the people in the city of Kampala, in the nation of Uganda, East Africa more than others elsewhere. No, it happened because we took time and gave glory and honor and thanks to Him, who sits on the throne, who lives forever and ever.

We saw God as Sovereign, able to solve all the problems, trials, lack and bondage in that area. We gave Him strength and glory. **"Give unto the Lord, O you mighty ones; give unto the Lord glory and strength. Give unto the Lord the glory due to His name; worship the Lord in the beauty of holiness." Psalms 29:1-2**

As you take time and minister to the Lord individually and co-operatively, the Lord God shall bring about changes in the house where you live, in your area of worship, in the town, city, and nation you stay. I heard the Lord say that in these last days He is going to shake nations with His power. *"Through the manifest presence of God, territories shall be taken for God, and much harvest for the kingdom shall be brought in."*

I also heard the Lord say that the confusion that the enemy plants in people's mind shall be dispelled.

"As My people minister to Me, the confusion sown among My people by religious spirits in numerous territories around the world shall be dispelled, and My people shall acknowledge Me as Lord and that besides there is no other, says the Lord God Almighty, and I do as I will, for with Me is salvation and strength, and I rule in the kingdoms of men and in My hand is power and might that no one is able to withstand Me, says the Lord."

{2}

WHAT IS MINISTERING TO GOD?

"As they ministered to the Lord and fasted, the Holy Spirit said, 'Now separate to me Barnabas and Saul for the work to which I have called them.'" Acts 13:2

I am going to tell you a little of my background which will be very helpful as we deal with this important question in the light of the Word of God.

I got born again in 1981 in Lummumba Hall, at Makerere University, Kampala, Uganda, East Africa. Up to that time I had been Catholic all my life. I was an altar boy in the Catholic Church from the time I was nine years. Every day after school, I would go and serve in the Catholic Church during their services in the evenings. I did this through St. Peter's Primary School in Kampala, Uganda. I also served as an altar boy when I joined St. Henry's College, Kitovu, in the city of Masaka, Uganda.

Now you have a glimpse of the religious background I came from. As an altar boy in the Catholic Church, I had an opportunity to be involved with nearly all the Mass activities. I want to sincerely let you know that by 1981 I didn't know that the Bible was for all people to read. I had been told by one of the priests that the reason why the layman should not read the Bible was because the lay believer can easily get confused reading it. So we were advised to stay away from the Bible.

As students at college, we studied all other subjects like mathematics, physics, geography, biology, chemistry, English, Luganda, technical drawing, art, accounts, literature, French, religious education, and I could very much excel in those. Most of the time I got straight A's, but unfortunately, I never had an opportunity to read the Bible of all the books.

Before I joined the university as a student of Engineering, I did do physics, mathematics, and chemistry at the advanced level. In all those subjects I could see the wisdom of God, for if someone is really sincere and not becoming lofty and then confused, the more you look and study these subjects, the more you have to acknowledge that the one who created all these laws must be very loving and all wise.

"**The Lord by wisdom founded the earth; by understanding He established the heavens; by His knowledge the depths were broken up, and clouds drop down the dew.**" **Proverbs 3:19-20**

Now, here I am with all this knowledge, scoring very high in my studies but void of the Word of God. Trying my best to serve God the way the Catholic Church then presented Him to us.

Surely, I never saw the power of God at all in those services and we did not expect God to move at all. The fact was that all they talked about was what happened during those days when the first apostles and Jesus Christ were on earth.

Thanks to God, these days many Catholics are getting born again and receiving the baptism of the Holy Spirit, as well as studying the Bible more fervently.

The Lord wanted me to clearly let you know my background that you may understand that I was ignorant about the Lord God like so many of us are until we get help.

My true encounter with the move of God was in 1980 when I escorted my aunt to a Christian meeting. My aunt came from what was called a protestant church. We were told that those kinds of churches were breakaways from the Catholic Church and were therefore in error. We had been advised to stay away from them, as well as the people walking around with the Bibles.

But what interested me to go with her was when she told us that the pastor conducting those meetings was doing miracles and wonders in the name of Jesus Christ. That people were being healed of all kinds of diseases and he could pray for people and they could get jobs, scholarships, etc.

Also that he could pray for people in the name of Jesus Christ and they could even be released from prisons. This was a very tough time in Uganda. We had just gone through a major war that deposed Idi Amin — a regime of terror. For this to be true, I knew in my heart there was a higher power involved. So I went with her to see with my own eyes whether it was true.

This preacher/pastor was preaching from the Bible. For everything he said, he gave a reference to it from the Bible. He had proof and substance for whatever he said.

Remember my academic culture or background most of the time we had to prove our argument scientifically, in line with the books of our disciplines. So when I observed this, I saw wisdom and understanding I had never seen before in my life. I had never seen this in all the years of my religion.

Even though, as an altar boy, I held out the Big Book referred to as a Vulgate that they read from during the Mass. I held it out, I mean. You stand in front of the Catholic priest during the Mass and hold up to him that Book with your two hands that he may read out of it. In the Catholic Church that is one of the most sacred moments, but unfortunately they never explained those readings in the light of the Bible, as I saw the preacher do.

Another thing that amazed me was how this man could know things about people without them telling him, and could even say something to people that would come to pass later. This I had from the testimonies of the people.

In fact, that was the first man to prophesy over my life in the name of Jesus Christ. All he spoke to me has come to pass. He pointed at me and said, *"Young man, God loves you; you shall preach the Gospel around the world. You shall pray for people and they shall get healed. You shall cast out demons. You shall build God churches and you shall operate in word of wisdom and word of knowledge as I am doing now. You shall write a number of books and you shall put the deepest truth in words by revelation knowledge, and shall draw men to the love of God."*

I remember, when he said that to me, I replied and said, "I am a Catholic." He didn't care. He just looked at me and smiled. Then he said to me, *"Before you reach home today you shall have a Bible in your hand."* And it happened exactly as he said.

I know you are thinking, *What is ministering to God?* That is where we are getting.

Though I saw all that, I didn't give my life to Jesus when the pastor made an altar call, for I was afraid of losing my religion! I loved my religion, though I had seen God so real.

Fortunately enough, after one year, through my friend at the university, I got born again. He showed me how to receive Jesus as my Lord and Savior and let me know, through the Scriptures in the Bible, that there was no way I could enter Heaven unless I became born again. **"Jesus answered and said to him, 'Most assuredly, I say to you, unless one is born again, he cannot see the Kingdom of God.'" John 3:3**

Also, the Word of God says in **Romans 10:9, "That if you confess with your mouth the Lord Jesus and believe in your heart that God has raised Him from the dead, you will be saved. For with the heart one believes unto righteousness, and with the mouth confession is made unto salvation!"**

That is exactly what I did that day, and that is what you need to do right now if you have never received Jesus in your life as your personal savior.

From that moment the Lord Jesus Christ came to see me through, as well as walk hand in hand with me in my journey of life. I no longer fight my battles alone, the Lord Jesus fights the battles with me and lights my path for me by His Word through the precious Holy Spirit who dwells in me — I am a new creation. I now tread under my feet the devils that used to walk all over me. **"Therefore, if anyone is in Christ, he is a new creation; old things have passed away, behold, all things have become new." II Corinthians 5:17**

I have good news for you: you can walk over the devils, religious devils, devils of divination, devils of lust, plus the powers of satan without them hurting you. **"Behold, I give you the authority to trample on serpents and scorpions, and over all the power of the enemy, and nothing shall by any means hurt you." Luke 10:19**

I very well know that a person needs to fulfill that part first as we continue our journey on the importance of ministering to God. I clearly know by the Spirit of God that this book is for every human being on the earth. This message from the Lord is for all God's people, for with knowledge one increases in strength. **"A wise man is strong, yes, a man of knowledge increases strength; for by wise counsel you will wage your own war, and in a multitude of counselor there is safety." Proverbs 24:5-6**

GOD HAS FEELINGS —
THE ESSENCE OF "WHAT IS MINISTERING TO GOD?"

One of the most important explanations for the very great manifestation of God's power in my life, the churches in which I have served as pastor (and I do pastor), in the crusades I have held around the world, is the understanding of that fact.

There are times in our services when God moves so strong I just get overwhelmed. I mean, when God manifests His Glory in our midst and every one partakes of it. When the presence of God is so strong that nearly everyone falls out under the power of God. **"And when I saw Him, I fell at His feet as dead. But He laid His right hand on me, saying to me, 'Do not be afraid; I am the First and the Last.'" Revelation 1:17**

That was the description of what happened to John when our Lord Jesus Christ revealed Himself in His Glory to him. I have seen that happen and in that kind of atmosphere charged with God's presence, so much happens. I have seen people just get healed without anyone touching them. People burst out speaking in "Tongues." Later they get very thankful when it is explained to them what they have received. Those are the moments when yokes break, burdens are removed, and lives get so much changed by the power of God.

These manifestations are available for individual lives and believers corporately, but one has to clearly understand that God can be touched by what we do and what we say and can respond accordingly. Here are a few incidental cases.

SOLOMON'S SPEECH PLEASES GOD

In the Book of Kings, the Word of God says that what Solomon said to God pleased Him. **"The speech pleased the Lord, that Solomon had asked this thing. Then God said to him: 'Because you have asked this thing, and have not asked long life for yourself, nor have asked riches for yourself, nor have asked the life of your enemies but have asked for yourself understanding to discern justice.'" I Kings 3:10-14**

Reading through those scriptures, you notice that most of the things we desire for our well-being in life are mentioned. Also, it is God who presented the offer to Solomon to ask, **"At Gibeon, the Lord appeared to Solomon in a dream by night; and God said, 'Ask! What shall I give you?'" I Kings 3:5**

So Solomon had the freedom to ask for anything, and he chose to do it in a way that would execute God's purpose for His people on earth and it pleased God. God was moved by his speech and he ended up getting even the things he hadn't asked for.

From these verses, we can clearly see that God is moved and pleased by what we say. Remember that God is a loving Father. **"For God so loved the world that He gave His only begotten Son, that whoever believes in Him should not perish but have everlasting life." John 3:16** Here we see God expressing affection towards the World, towards us as individuals. GOD LOVES YOU!

IN GENESIS WE SEE THAT GOD BECAME GRIEVED OVER THE WICKEDNESS OF MAN

"Then the Lord saw that the wickedness of man was great in the earth, and that every intent of the thoughts of his heart was only evil continually. And the Lord was sorry that He had made man on the earth, and He was grieved in His heart." Genesis 6:5-6

GOD SMELLS A SOOTHING AROMA

In Genesis, the Lord smelled a soothing aroma from the burnt offerings on the altar by Noah. **"Then Noah built an altar to the Lord, and took of every clean animal and of every clean bird, and offered burnt offerings on the altar. And the Lord smelled a soothing aroma. Then the Lord said in His heart, 'I will never again curse the ground for man's sake, although the imagination of man's heart is evil from his youth; nor will I again destroy every living thing as I have done.'" Genesis 8:20-21**

GOD RESPONDS TO HIS PEOPLE'S
SORROWS AND OPPRESSION

In Exodus 3, God responds to the cries of His people in Egypt and says He knows their sorrows. **"And the Lord said: 'I have surely seen the oppression of My people who are in Egypt, and have heard their cry because of their taskmasters, for I know their sorrows.'" Exodus 3:7**

GOD LOVES

In Leviticus, Chapter 19, you hear the heartbeat of God as a loving Father, one who feels and knows what it is like to not be affectionate. **"You shall not hate your brother in your heart. You shall surely rebuke your neighbor, and not bear sin because of him. You shall not take vengeance, nor bear any grudge against the children of your people, but you shall love your neighbor as yourself: I am the Lord." Leviticus 19:17-18**

God created us in His image. We can laugh, we can know when we are being blessed, and we do appreciate being loved as well as honored. We are affected positively when God loves us and blesses us. Likewise, God responds to the way we treat Him and relate with Him. GOD HAS FEELINGS.

GOD CAN FEEL REJECTION

In Numbers 14, God experienced rejection when the behavior of the children of Israel expressed doubt of who God is and what He can do. **"Then the Lord said to Moses, 'How long will these people reject Me? How long will they not believe Me, with all the signs which I have performed among them? I will strike them with the pestilence and disinherit them, and I will make of you a nation greater and mightier than they.'"** **Numbers 14:11-12.**

The last part of the twelfth verse shows that the words of those people, plus their behavior did not please God at all. These people were only concerned about themselves and they placed their challenges and fears above God's sure promise of salvation. Indirectly, they were saying, "God, you cannot manage this." And that is rejection.

WHAT IS MINISTERING TO GOD?

Ministering to God is taking the time and proclaiming to Him, willingly, lovingly, and in faith, what through His Word He says He is. Following are two examples.

GOD IS ALMIGHTY

When you say to God, "Lord, You are Almighty," you are glorifying God and proclaiming to Him, as well a establishing the fact that God is Almighty. THIS IS MINISTERING TO HIM. **"When Abram was ninety-nine years old, the Lord appeared to Abram and said to him, 'I am Almighty God; Walk before me and be blameless.'" Genesis 17:1**

GOD IS HOLY

When you say to God, "Lord, You are Holy," THAT IS MINISTERING TO HIM. You are acknowledging His holiness. **"And the Lord spoke to Moses, saying, 'Speak to all the congregation of the children of Israel, and say to them: "you shall be Holy, for I the Lord Your God is Holy."'" Leviticus 19:1-2**

The wonderful thing about it is, when we take time and proclaim what He is, despite our conditions or circumstances around us, whether they are good or bad a beautiful aroma of trust and faith is carried along our words to the heart of God — and in that God is blessed!

TRUE INTEGRITY MINISTERS TO GOD AT ALL TIMES

Job's affection towards God, by loving and proclaiming Him blessed, even after hearing all the bad news, from the messengers who escaped from the different scenes of loss, is referred to as integrity.

"Then the Lord said to satan, 'Have you considered my servant Job, that there is none like him on the earth, a blameless and upright man, one who fears God and shuns evil? And still he holds fast to his integrity, although you incited me against him, to destroy him without cause.'" Job 2:3

In Job's case, it is clear that the devil's intention was to move him to curse God. The wicked one wanted Job to respond to God out of disappointment, anger, unbelief, or to totally stop worshipping God. But Job didn't do that. He went on giving God glory and honor and this is where you see Job's strength — his ability to worship, that is, to minister, to God — insisting that God is blessed even though, in the natural Job was surrounded by grief. "Then Job arose, tore his robe, and shaved his head, and he fell to the ground and worshiped, and he said, 'Naked I came from my mother's womb, and naked shall I return there. The Lord gave; the Lord has taken away; blessed be the name of the Lord.'" Job 1:20-21

This is what we did in the eastern side of Kampala City, Uganda. Within that area, amidst all the challenges from the religious spirits, the spirits of sorcery, and some people, who were against the proclamation of God's Word in that area, plus the living conditions not being very good by then in Kamwokya, we still confessed and acknowledged God, as well as declared in the heavens that He is what He says He is.

The effect of this was tremendous, for God responded so powerfully. Healings, salvation, deliverance, and material blessings, followed. The devils screamed as the invisible fire of God consumed them. They left people's lives crying aloud because the hand of God was strong against them. In most of our services, before I even started binding the enemy and casting him out, God was already dealing with him.

MINISTERING TO GOD
IS A POSITION OF STRENGTH

"But Samuel ministered before the Lord, even as a child, wearing a linen ephod." I Samuel 2:18

Beloved, this is what this book is about. God wants to get you in a place of power, miracles, wonders and signs in Him. It is a position of strength in God. This is where Jesus steps in the situation and all the enemies' work gets destroyed by the Holy Spirit. **"How God anointed Jesus of Nazareth with the Holy Spirit and with power, who went about doing good and healing all who were oppressed by the devil, for God was with Him." Acts 10:38**

In this position of coming to God with sounds of praise to Him, the Lord answers before you call and He manifests His beautiful glory while you are still speaking. **"It shall come to pass that before they call, I will answer; and while they are still speaking, I will hear." Isaiah 65:24**

Awesome! I want to tell you that is a very strong place in God we all need to be in as a body of Christ. Churches can operate at that level. Your individual life can experience that grace. That is the plateau the Holy Spirit is bringing you to right now!

There are times in our services, as we take time to minister to God, the entire congregation gets caught up in the beautiful, powerful, blessed presence of God. It is a wonderful experience. People get touched and blessed in this atmosphere charged with God's tangible presence. People receive wisdom to deal with day-to-day challenges of life. They also get very strengthened in their inner man. They get very bold.

"And when they had prayed, the place where they were assembled together was shaken, and they were all filled with the Holy Spirit, and they spoke the Word of God with boldness." Acts 4:31

PROPHETIC WORD TO YOU

I hear the Lord say, **"*As you minister to me,*"** says the Lord, "*and as you take time to worship Me,*" says the Lord God Almighty, "*I will bring you to places of peace you have never experienced in your life. I will fill your being with My wisdom,* "says the Lord, "*and I will cause My favor to rest on you and My presence shall go with you. I will cause you to inherit the wealth of the wicked and you shall know My riches,*" says the Lord God, "*and your life shall bear much fruit, for many shall come to the knowledge of the saving grace of my Son, Jesus Christ, through your life,*" says the Lord God Almighty.

PROPHETIC WORD TO CHURCH LEADERSHIP

"*Pastors, prophets, teachers, evangelists, apostles, time has come to equip My people with divine strength, divine wisdom, through the act of ministering to the Lord. Show My people how to ascribe to Me glory, honor and majesty,*" says the Lord. "*For as they honor Me, they shall experience Honor; as they glorify My name, they shall know My glory,*" says the Lord, "*For My mountain shall be established on the top of the mountains, and shall be exalted above the hills; and all nations shall flow to it. Many people shall come and say, 'Come, let us go up to the mountain of the Lord, to the house of the God of Jacob, He will teach us His ways and we shall walk in His paths, for the mouth of the Lord has spoken.'*"

TEN THOUSAND PEOPLE WITHIN A TWO SQUARE MILE RADIUS OF OUR CHURCH GET BORN AGAIN

We won from fifty to one-hundred-fifty people to the Lord every day. Most of them were a result of a one-to-one witnessing by the saints who attended the church services and took time to minister to the Lord.

They went out of the services with the presence of God all over them. This is like dipping someone in water, then letting him loose all wet. The Glory of the Lord was all over them and it could be felt and seen!

The spirit of unbelief, which plays a great deal in holding people away from the Word of God, could not stand against this anointing on the Lord's people.

There is a year, 1994, when we got 10,000 people born again within a two square mile radius of our church, Christian Faith Center, in the nation of Uganda.

One of the other things which gave us such dominion over the territory was my taking time as the pastor, or under-shepherd, of God's people to teach them how to minister to God.

Another factor was the people accepting and taking seriously what I showed them in the Word concerning the need to minister to God, and understanding that God is touched and pleased by us honoring Him and blessing Him.

As a servant of the Lord, an apostle of Jesus Christ through the will of God, I exhort you to start taking time and going to God in the name of Jesus Christ and lovingly, faithfully showering Him with blessings in your heart and by your mouth, proclaiming and establishing in the hearing of the invisible and visible that He is what He says He is.

When you do this, you shall prosper. **"So they rose early in the morning and went out into the wilderness of Tekoa, and as they went out, Jehoshaphat stood and said, 'Hear me, O Judah and you inhabitants of Jerusalem: believe in the Lord your God, and you shall be established, believe His prophets and you shall prosper.'" II Chronicles 20:20**

What I am sharing with you here has brought prosperity to my ministry, the churches I have founded, the people who have obeyed and responded to this revelation in God's Word. People have been set free from all kinds of diseases, yokes have been broken and burdens have been removed off their lives.

As I was writing this book, a man of God was talking to me from Atlanta, Georgia, U.S.A. This man of God had been pastoring for some time and now he had moved to that location. He needed a property to carry out church services.

Suddenly, as he was talking to me, God spoke these words, *"Tell him to look around that area. There is a church building which is empty. The people who had it could not keep it any longer, for their congregation instead of growing had dwindled. He shall find it and it will be his next church building."*

This pastor and evangelist believed what I told him and searched the area. Within four days, he found the property and got it for church. God is omniscient — all knowing! God has given me an opportunity to pray for and counsel with many people. There were times when I could pray with and for about fifteen people every day. These people were coming from all over the nation of Uganda, from different places.

When people recognize that God's hand is on you, manifested in the anointing flowing through your life, miracles done by God through you, wisdom of the Holy Spirit, healings done by our Lord Jesus Christ through your life, kindness, compassion, patience, love shed in your heart by the Holy Spirit, they will always come to you for help. People can recognize God in your life or church. Because of this, I get to meet a lot of people. This happens in whatever country I go and this is going to start happening to you, for people are going to respond to the glory of God on your life. You should be ready to help them.

"But sanctify the Lord God in your hearts, and always be ready to give a defense to everyone who asks you a reason for the hope that is in you, with meekness and fear." I Peter 3:15

MOSLEM TOUCHED BY GOD AS SHE MINISTERED TO HIM IN THE NAME OF OUR LORD JESUS CHRIST

One day, about 10 o'clock in the morning, I was in my office at the church in Uganda. Normally I would be in the office by 6 o'clock early morning for already by that time people would be arriving for God's counsel and prayer, as they wanted to see me.

That morning, among those who came was a Moslem woman. This woman was around forty-nine years, and she was having a sickness in her body of a form very difficult for even the doctors to describe. It was as if something was moving in her body. In the natural, she felt a bad force in her back that would move up and down her and this could cause uneasiness in her life as well as a lot of pain. This had been happening to her since she was seventeen years old. She had tried hospitals, witch doctors, the Imams of the Islam faith, for help but they couldn't help her.

Many described it as a blood condition that could lead to death any time.

Just looking at her, you could see she was not happy. Sometimes it would feel as if someone tied something tightly around her chest. She described to me her condition and I let her know that with God nothing is too hard. **"Behold, I am the Lord, the God of all flesh. Is there anything too hard for me?" Jeremiah 32:27**

This woman was tired of that condition. Though she had been brought up a Moslem, she was ready to do anything if it could touch God to help her. Remember, this woman had been taught in her religion that God has no Son and can't have one. That Jesus Christ was just a prophet and Mohammed was the last prophet. She was also preached to in the Mosque that there can't be three persons in God, so Christianity is false.

As she sat before me, the Holy Spirit spoke to me and said, *"Tell her to stand up and raise her hands to heaven, and guide her in ministering to God in the name of Jesus Christ."* That is exactly what I told her to do, well enough that she listened and repeated after me these words of worship:

"Father, I say, in the name of Jesus Christ, that you are worthy. In the name of your Son, Jesus Christ, I say that you are holy. Holy art thou, Lord God; righteous art thou, Lord God. Might is with thee, oh Lord, and deliverance comes now from You.

No yoke, no burden, no captivity, for in Jesus Christ, Your Son, you set people free."

While she was still speaking, something wonderful happened. Suddenly the Lord God touched her! I saw her whole body vibrating under the power of God and the glory of God was so much that she could not stand any more.

Thank God for the catchers that help us when we are ministering. They were already behind her and helped her to lie down for she could not hold herself up due to the power of God.

Next, the demons that were tormenting her started screaming aloud that the fire of God was burning them. I could not see that fire by the naked eye, but the way the devils were crying for mercy, you could know that surely there was an invisible furnace in the place. I cast them out in the name of Jesus Christ.

When this large, tall woman rose up after fifteen minutes, she was totally healed. The next thing she asked me was, "What must I do to become a Christian?"

I led her in the prayer of salvation and as she continued giving glory, honor, power, and thanksgiving to God Almighty, she suddenly started speaking in tongues as the Holy Spirit gave her utterance.

I did not even lay hands on her. It was like what took place when Peter was preaching in the house of Cornelius.

"While Peter was still speaking these words the Holy Spirit fell upon all those who heard the Word. And those of the circumcision who believed were astonished, as many as came with Peter, because the gift of the Holy Spirit had been poured out on the Gentiles also. For they heard them speak with tongues and magnify God." Acts 10:44-46

This is exactly what happened to this woman, newly converted from Islam to Christianity.

As she was speaking those words, magnifying and glorifying God, in trust and love, God baptized her in the Holy Spirit! This woman is still born again as I write this book. She goes to a church in Uganda and she is one of the intercessors in the church.

Thanks to God, she didn't let her religious background cheat her out of God's blessings. **"Let no one cheat you of your reward, taking delight in false humility and worship of angels, intruding into those things which he has not seen, vainly puffed up by his fleshly mind, and not holding fast to the head, from whom all the body, nourished and knit together by joints and ligaments, grows with the increase that is from God." Colossians 2:18-19**

There is increase from God for our lives, for the churches, and for the people around us. I always get excited when I see people getting blessed like this. When we minister to God, He gets pleased.

When we declare before God and establish the fact through our utterance by mouth and in our heart that He is God and the One who made all things, we are ministering to Him. This is what the disciples did in **Acts 4:24 "So when they heard that, they raised their voice to God with one accord and said, 'Lord, you are God, who made heaven and earth and the sea, and all that is in them.'"**

When you look at this part of prayer, you notice that they are confessing, proclaiming, as well as acknowledging that He is the Creator. They declared to Him that He made the heaven, earth and sea.

No wonder the place where they were assembled together was shaken, for they acknowledged the greatness of God amidst the threats of the Sanhedrin. In love, trust and faith they held their integrity toward God and maintained the fact that God is what He says He is in His Word. What He says belongs to Him is so. This way, they pleased God, for that is an act of faith. **"But without faith it is impossible to please him, for he who comes to God must believe that He is, and that he is a rewarder of those who diligently seek him."**
Hebrews 11:6

There is something else I would like you to notice: they were talking to God directly, not telling someone else about God.

The ministering to God I am talking about here is what you can do even in your closet, for in Him we live. **"For in Him we live and move and have our being, as also some of your own poets have said, 'For we are also His offspring.'"** Acts 17:28

It is also very important for you to attend a Bible-believing, teaching Church, as well as take time to read the Bible. **"This Book of the Law shall not depart from your mouth, but you shall meditate in it day and night, that you may observe to do according to all that is written in it. For then you will make your way prosperous, and then you will have good success."** Joshua 1:8 Then you can be able to celebrate God within His Will.

What I am sharing with you has enabled me to help a lot of people get in the tangible manifested presence of God. People have come to me with what they felt were insurmountable problems, when all they were seeing and smelling was the enemy. Most of the time the Holy Spirit would quickly guide me by the Word of God to bring them to the scriptures that reveal God's omnipotence and omniscience, then I could lead them into the beauty of ministering to God, with words like these:

"The earth is thine, Lord, and all its fullness. The world and those who dwell therein." **"The earth is the Lord's, and all its fullness, the world and those who dwell therein."** **Psalm 24:1** *"All the houses are yours, Lord, the roads are thine, the vehicles are yours, mighty one. All the jobs are thine, the schools are yours, Father, the hospitals are thine, and I thank you for all these in the name of Jesus."* **"Who has preceded me, that I should pay him? Everything under heaven is mine."** **Job 41:11** *"Lord God, all the money is thine, the dollar is thine, the shilling (Ugandan currency) is thine"* **"'The silver is mine, and the gold is mine,' says the Lord of Hosts."** **Haggai 2:8** *"Father, the cattle on a thousand hills is thine, all the properties are thine and all the birds that fly in the air."* **"I will not take a bull from your House, nor goats out of your folds. For every beast of the forest is mine, and the cattle on a thousand hills. I know all the birds of the mountains. And the wild beasts of the field are mine. If I were hungry, I would not tell you; for the world is mine, and all its fullness."**
Psalms 50:9-12

In doing so, you are declaring, proclaiming, acknowledging that all things belong to God. This pleases Him and He responds mightily in love and power.

THE WHOLE FAMILY TOUCHED BY
THE POWER OF GOD

A family came to see me at the church office, the father, mother and three of their children. The children were not yet baptized in the Holy Spirit with evidence of speaking in tongues. The father hadn't received the gift of the Holy Spirit either. It was only the mother that was baptized in the Holy Spirit.

She had told them about the mighty things the Lord was doing in our meetings. So they decided to come to see me. They had many questions.

This man was attending a church that believed in salvation, that unless one is born again he or she cannot see the Kingdom of God. **"Jesus answered and said to him, 'Most assuredly, I say to you, unless one is born again, he cannot see the Kingdom of God.'" John 3:3** But they basically stopped right there at receiving Jesus as a personal Savior.

They never knew the power of God manifest. Their way of coming to God was mostly explaining to Him the troubles and problems going on in the earth. They spent a lot of time in their services fighting the devils, binding everything they would bind. Their life was a life of much struggle to get God to move, and they had very little time of ministering to the Lord in their midst.

They had not embraced the doctrine of the baptism in the Holy Spirit with the evidence of speaking in tongues. They had also become more closed into themselves than open to the public, to come and receive from the Lord.

They were more on the defensive, instead of the offensive, and they lacked power to witness. **"But you shall receive power when the Holy Spirit comes upon you; and you shall be witnesses to me in Jerusalem, in all Judea and Samaria, and to the end of the earth."** Acts 1:8

When these people came before me, I led them into the presence of the Lord. As we corporately gave glory, honor and thanks to Him who sits on the throne, who created the heavens and the earth, and with whom nothing is too difficult, the place was filled with the Glory of God. The Glory of God was so beautifully upon all of them, they couldn't stay on the chairs on which they sat — thank God for the catchers who helped them lie down. The Lord was just in our midst. His presence was tangible.

I hadn't placed my hands on any of them, yet what followed was most beautiful. The man and his children started speaking in tongues. One of his children got instantly healed of a heart condition.

These people continued in the presence of the Lord for about thirty minutes. They didn't want to move out of my office, for what they experienced was so precious to them.

All the arguments received and learned from the people who had told them they didn't need the Baptism of the Holy Spirit evaporated, for obedience was fulfilled in that aspect — they won that war! **"For though we walk in the flesh, we do not war according to the flesh. For the weapons of our warfare are not carnal but mighty in God for pulling down strongholds, casting down arguments and every high thing that exalts itself against the knowledge of God, bringing every thought into captivity to the obedience of Christ, and being ready to punish all disobedience when your obedience is fulfilled." II Corinthians 10:3-6**

This is what we need today. This is what a number of churches around the world need so they may be effective in the area of their assignment.

What amazed them was the fact that I didn't spend time fighting devils nor spend time explaining to God what needed to be done.

Something also very astonishing to them was that they could receive the Baptism of the Holy Spirit, with evidence of speaking in tongues, without me struggling over them and without anybody laying hands on them. I am sure the Lord saw their contrite hearts. **"But on this one will I look. On him who is poor and a contrite spirit, and who trembles at My Word." Isaiah 66:2**

That is exactly what they did. They took seriously the instructions I gave them by the Spirit of God and moved from the position of fleshly power and might and took on the Lord's way. **"So he answered and said to me: 'This is the Word of the Lord to Zerubbabel: "Not by might nor by power, but by my Spirit," says the Lord of Hosts.'" Zechariah 4:6**

One of the greatest assignments of religious devils is to wear you out so that you stop seeking God. They put obstacles in your way to complicate your Christian walk. They are very contributive to Christian lives void of power and the anointing of God, lives and services that do not reflect the Kingdom of God.

The wicked one knows that if he can draw you to concentrate on the challenges of life, instead of the Lord over challenges, then your life can't be pleasing to God. In fact, the churches, plus individual lives, just diminish instead of increasing. People get tired of just words alone without power. **"For the Kingdom of God is not in word but in power."**

I Corinthians 4:20 It takes God working with us, in us and through us to fulfill the Great Commission of reaching the World with the Gospel.

PROPHETIC WORD TO YOU

"Arise in this revelation and minister to the Lord God Almighty. Be strong and of good courage, do not be afraid, nor be dismayed, for the Lord is with you wherever you go and the Lord is bringing you to your place in Him," says the Lord. *"And as you take time in the Name of my Son, Jesus Christ, to minister to Me, I will make you wise."* Says the Lord, *"I will make you rich."* Says the Lord God Almighty, *"And what used to look like big mountains before you I will cause you to walk over them like ant hills. Sound shall be your mind and healthy shall by your body."*

When you pray to the Lord saying, **"Ah, Lord God! Behold, you have made the heavens and the earth by your great power and outstretched arm. There is nothing too hard for you. You show loving kindness to thousands, and repay the iniquity of the fathers into the bosom of their children after them - The great, the mighty God, whose name is the Lord of Hosts. You are great in counsel and mighty in work"**

Jeremiah 32:17-19, this is ministering to the Lord.

You are acknowledging the works of the Lord in the heavens and on the earth. You are proclaiming and establishing the fact that those mighty works of love, mercy, and kindness proceed from Him and Him alone. Coming to God this way blesses Him. His heart is touched. You please Him and then He reveals His works even more.

Our services in Kamwokya carried so much power that many preachers got interested in what was happening. A number of pastors, teachers, prophets, evangelists, apostles and other church leaders started to come to our church services to find out exactly what was happening.

Many times, I could be standing by the pulpit, just busy ascribing greatness to the Lord God Almighty in the name of our Lord Jesus Christ, and the Lord would simultaneously heal the people.

The Lord touched the people right where they were in their seats and He let me know by His Spirit what He had done so that I could let the congregation know.

For example, the Lord could let me know that He has just healed someone of AIDS, tumor, headaches, back pain and as I was saying these things, those people were already experiencing God's healing power going through their bodies like electricity. And to some, it was like a great healing warmth, for others, whatever was holding them in torment they felt it snap.

Others, as they ministered to the Lord, ended up receiving the baptism of the Holy Spirit with the evidence of speaking in tongues.

My brother/my sister, the power of God was so much among the people that devils left very fast, screaming and crying loudly.

PASTOR AND HIS CHURCHES REVIVED

During one of our services, a pastor came with his associates from a church forty miles from Kampala. This man had been pastoring for the last thirty-seven years and had started seven churches in different places. They had told him that there was a young man of God, around twenty-seven years of age, pastoring a church in Kamwokya, called Christian Faith Center. And the church has been in the area for only two years, but the entire nation is being affected by what the Lord is doing with him.

Some members of his church had visited and attended our services and went away full of joy, telling what great things the Lord had done for them.

That day, as I was praying for other people, this man of God said to me, "Please pray for me. I need a touch from the Lord." What I did was just to ask him to testify first about what he had seen the Lord do in that service.

Amazingly, when this man of God, so happy and astonished, started to thankfully say out what he had just witnessed in the service, as he was still speaking, the power of God fell on him and the associates who came with him! The Lord touched them so beautifully they were literally vibrating under the anointing.

That day religious yokes were broken off them. The pastor was healed of a chest problem from which he had suffered for five years. One associate's hearing was restored and the spirit of heaviness that had weighed on the pastor for five years lifted off completely.

This man, in his testimony, said that what amazed him was the fact that we took time to give the Lord glory, honor, and strength. **"Give unto the Lord, O you mighty ones, Give unto the Lord glory and strength. Give unto the Lord the glory due to his name; worship the Lord in the beauty of Holiness." Psalms 29:1-2**

This pastor said that we behaved as if the devil was under our feet and we regarded his words as nothing in the light of God's presence. Many times devils try to argue back when commanded to leave people's lives, but they can be silenced in the name of Jesus, and that is exactly what we did to them.

From that day on, the pastor and his associates entered another place in God. They moved to another glory plateau with the Lord Almighty and when they returned to their churches everything changed. They started teaching the believers how to take some time and give unto the Lord God the glory due to His name. Consequently, their churches grew and increased in numbers.

WHAT IS MINISTERING TO THE LORD?

Ministering to God is giving unto the Lord glory and strength through the name of His Son, Jesus Christ.

That is what was done in the church at Antioch. **"Now in the church that was at Antioch there were certain prophets and teachers: Barnabas, Simeon, who was called Niger, Lucius of Cyrene, Manaen who had been brought up with Herod the tetrarch and Saul. As they ministered to the Lord and fasted, the Holy Spirit said, 'Now separate to me Barnabas and Saul for the work to which I have called them.'" Acts 13:1-2**

In an atmosphere charged with proclamation of what God is and what He owns, plus what he has done and is doing, many times the Holy Spirit speaks to his people individually and corporately.

The Holy Spirit is pointing out assignments placed on people's lives by God and gifts of revelation knowledge are functional: tongues and interpretation, word of knowledge, word of wisdom, prophecy. Things get confirmed to people's lives. People get open visions as well.

Many times in this kind of environment/atmosphere I have supernaturally known the offices to which God has called some people to function in and pointed them out by the Spirit of God.

Nearly all those the Lord permitted me to point out by His spirit are now pastoring churches around the World, others are prophets, very anointed, and others are teachers, and other are evangelists.

Others are apostles, as I am, and have planted a number of churches already and also go around strengthening existing churches, bringing some back to the true foundation — JESUS CHRIST.

GOD REVEALS A PASTORAL CALL
ON A BELIEVER'S LIFE

I remember one tall man who started coming to our church services. He lived 275 miles away from Kampala. He had come to visit his relatives and they encouraged him to come to church every day.

We were holding services every day in the evenings. This man attended nearly all our services for a year. When he first attended our church he was amazed at what he saw happening.

Though he had been born again for six years, he had never been in such services charged with God's power. Services where people were getting born again every day, healed, blessed with wisdom, from the Lord Almighty.

He didn't even know about the anointing of God that breaks yokes.

This man was a businessman. He was a trader. During one Sunday morning service, I was ministering before the people of God and the Lord gave me a word for this man. The Lord said to him, by my mouth, that He called him to stand in the office of a pastor and a teacher. The Lord said He would show him a place to begin the church. All this came to pass.

I visited his church in 1995. It was a beautiful church building with nice church people and God's presence was in that place. He also ended up owning a grocery store in that area.

You can do all things through Christ who strengthens you. **"I can do all things through Christ who strengthens me." Philippians 4:13.** You can minister to God! You can get over all your religious limitations.

God can minister to you and through you healing, protection, provision, joy, peace, wisdom, counsel, favor, humility and authority.

Stir yourself up in God and get hold of God's might in the name of Jesus Christ. That is what I did by the grace of God. You can do it too.

My Catholic background didn't show me this, but in my heart I had a witness, or knowing, that if God is real and is what I hear Him to be, His power could still be manifested among His people today. As I studied the Holy Scriptures, I found this:

"Behold, the Lord's hand is not shortened, that it cannot save; nor His ear heavy that it cannot hear. But your iniquities have separated you from your God; and your sins have hidden His face from you, so He will not hear."
Isaiah 59:1-2.

When we reject God's Word, concerning our fellowship with Him through His son Jesus Christ, then we have rejected the counsel of God. When we reject the counsel of God, revealed in the Bible, we end up living a very difficult life, a religious life that is void of God's power and glory.

Each one of us is responsible for what we give to our ears to hear and our eyes to see. Make sure you get to know the Word of God personally. Read the Bible and help others to move forward in God. Many people will be helped through your obedience as you arise and shine in God. "Arise, shine; for your light has come! And the glory of the Lord is risen upon you."
Isaiah 60:1.

FOR GOD GIVES
WISDOM AND KNOWLEDGE
AND
JOY TO A MAN
WHO IS GOOD IN HIS SIGHT;
BUT TO THE SINNER
HE GIVES THE WORK
OF GATHERING
AND
COLLECTING,
THAT HE MAY GIVE
TO HIM WHO IS GOOD
BEFORE GOD.
THIS ALSO
IS
VANITY AND GRASPING
FOR THE WIND.
ECCLESIASTES 2:26

{3}

MINISTERING TO GOD

Key To A Financially Prosperous Life/Church Filled With God's Power, Miracles, Wonders, and Signs

"And He said to them, 'Go into all the world and preach the Gospel to every creature. He who believes and is baptized will be saved; but he who does not believe will be condemned. And these signs will follow those who believe: in My name they will cast out demons; they will speak with new tongues; they will take up serpents; and if they drink anything deadly, it will by no means hurt them; they will lay hands on the sick, and they will recover.'" Mark 16:15-18

Before we talk about any other kind of prosperity, we need to have this area clarified. For what the Lord is talking about here you cannot buy with money, these signs are wrought by God through the lives of believers. This is part of what happens when someone is living a spirit-filled life.

A spirit-filled life glorifies Jesus Christ. A spirit-filled life gives glory and honor to the Lord God Almighty, and proclaims Him Lord over all for that is what the Holy Spirit brings about. **"He will glorify me, for He will take of what is mine and declare it to you." John 16:14**

When your desire is to glorify Jesus Christ, always remember the third person of the God Head, the Holy Spirit, will enjoy manifesting the Works of God through your life, for your desire is in agreement with His purpose and in that way you are in agreement with Him. **"Can two walk together, unless they are agreed?" Amos 3:3**

The Holy Spirit is God Himself and whatever He does has to prosper. He loves manifesting signs, wonders, miracles and the power of God through people who love God, those who would take time to ascribe greatness and honor to God, people who take time to acknowledge that all power and real authority belongs to the Lord God Almighty, people who are ready to glorify the Lord God of miracles, wonders and signs, instead of the signs, miracles and wonders of the Lord. Because the latter can result in confusion, and many times flesh can try to take the glory, this can result in the Lord withdrawing His manifestations from our lives.

Jesus died for souls, for people. When souls are won through your life, you are living a prosperous life, a life which is not barren, for you are giving birth to spiritual babies. This is the number one reason why you need the power of God manifest through your life.

The more you draw near to God through your taking time and ministering to God, the more He draws near to you and the more the glory of the Lord increases on your life. **"Therefore submit to God. Resist the devil and he will flee from you. Draw near to God and He will draw near to you. Cleanse your hands, you sinners; and purify your hearts, you double-minded." James 4:7-8.**

When God's glory is on you strong, it disarms the evil forces and powers that hold back people in unbelief, and then it is easier to witness to them with the blinders off. It now rests on their free will to choose Christ, for the doors and chains that have been holding them back fall off due to God's glory on your life. In this way, you can have good success in winning the lost.

What I am telling you in this book I have experienced practically and I have heard saints expressing surprise at how the people responded to the Gospel of salvation as they witnessed to the different individuals they met during day to day activities.

It is the anointing of God on their lives that makes a difference.

We had great success winning souls through the saints in our church. Those who stepped out and went for souls could win up to ten souls individually. That is how we won fifty to a hundred lost souls every day, through individual members attending our services who took time to give unto God glory, honor, and strength.

GRANDMA MARY –
VERY PROSPEROUS IN WINNING SOULS

I remember a certain grandma by the name of Mary.
She loved the Lord and she attended nearly every service we had in Kamwokya Christian Faith Center.

She used to take time and just say, "I give You the Glory, Lord. Thou who made the heavens and the earth." **"In the beginning God created the Heavens and the Earth." Genesis 1:1** "You are so powerful, Lord God, thou who gave us the authority to trample on serpents and scorpions, and over all the power of the enemy and nothing shall hurt us by any means." **"Behold, I give you the authority to trample on serpents and scorpions, and over all the power of the enemy, and nothing shall by any means hurt you." Luke 10:19** "Lord God, I thank you in the name of Jesus for the sins which follow us as we preach the Gospel to the people. I give you all the glory, thou, who empowers us to win souls."

"And these signs will follow those who believe: in My name, they will cast out demons; they will speak with new tongues; they will take up serpents; and if they drink anything deadly, it will by no means hurt them; they will lay hands on the sick, and they will recover." Mark 16:17-18 "Father, I present to you all the people I am going to witness to today in the name of Jesus. I present them to you, thou who is able to remove by your power anything holding them and burdening their lives, and Lord, at least grant me to win ten souls today. Thou, O'Lord, art the God of all flesh, to whom nothing is too difficult." **"Behold, I am the Lord, the God of all flesh. Is there anything too hard for me?" Jeremiah 32:27**

Nearly all the time this 70-year-old grandmother prayed, God revealed His tangible presence to her. The Lord would touch her so strongly that you could see the power of God all over her. She would be filled with the Holy Spirit and get very bold. **"And when they had prayed, the place where they were assembled together was shaken; and they were all filled with the Holy Spirit, and they spoke the Word of God with boldness." Acts 4:31**

Grandma Mary spoke Luganda, which is a Ugandan language. She went out after the souls and always got something like ten to twenty people born again every day. Signs and wonders followed her and unbelievers would ask her to pray for healing of their loved ones. Many times when they recovered, they would look for her so she may tell them the secret of God's power in her life. She would end up leading them to the prayer of salvation. **"That if you confess with your mouth the Lord Jesus and believe in your heart that God has raised Him from the dead, you will be saved." Romans 10:9**

There is something about a life that experiences a flesh-touch from the Lord God Almighty. God energizes that life and affects it to go forward in that divine empowerment and do the works of Jesus Christ. Even in circumstances that look so contrary. Individuals tend to be very productive for God, and they execute God's will on Earth. Even worldly people, when they look on them, sense and see the glory of God on them.

When you spend time in God's presence, as Moses did in Exodus, God's glory will be manifested on you. **"Now it was so, when Moses came down from Mount Sinai (and the two tablets of the testimony were in Moses's hand when he came   down from the mountain), that Moses did not know that the skin of his face shone while he talked with Him. So when Aaron and all the children of Israel saw Moses, behold, the skin of his face shone, and they were afraid to come near him." Exodus 34:29-30** In this case the glory of the Lord was on Moses's face and it could be seen as well as felt.

There are many times when the Holy Spirit has manifested his gifts through different people in our services as we ministered to God, I Corinthians 12 became so real to us. In this kind of atmosphere God's children tend to flow easier with the Holy Spirit.

Tongues and interpretation, Word of Wisdom, Word of Knowledge, and discernment in the spirit, comes forth the Holy Spirit moves on different people as He wills and we all end up blessed through these supernatural manifestations, the gifts of the Holy Spirit.

God also reveals to people His will concerning the day- to-day affairs, things concerning how to run their businesses, they just know what to do. Many times, they get a divine revelation and know in their spirit what they need to do.

When they do what has been revealed to them by God, they prosper. **"For the Word of God is living and powerful, and sharper than any two edged sword, piercing even to the division of soul and spirit, and of joints and marrow, and is a discerner of the thoughts and intents of the heart."**
Hebrews 4:12.

God's Word is His Will and the Bible makes it very clear that when God speaks, or when God's Word comes to you, it can be so penetrating that all your being gets filled with the knowledge of what God says.

This kind of manifestation happens to me many times when I am ministering. God gives me a Word for individual lives as well as the people in the hearing of my voice.

Most of the time, I just look at a person and know that person is suffering from a disease in a certain place of his/her body. As I speak forth what I know, by the spirit of God, it is always so and I see God healing people instantly.

There are times, when God lets me know about the challenges individuals are going through and then reveals His wisdom for the solution of those seemingly impossible situations, and it happens exactly as God revealed it.

God revealed to me the callings on people's lives and it has come to pass exactly as I spoke to them by His spirit. A number of them are now operating strongly in the offices of apostle, prophet, evangelist, teacher, pastor.

You may say *how do you know this? Do you know this because you are a preacher?* No. I just know. Many times I don't hear an audible voice, I just know. I only seek to do His will and He promised, **"If anyone wills to do His Will, he shall know concerning the doctrine, whether it is from God or whether I speak on my own authority." John 7:17**

As you step out to minister to God, God will start revealing to you what you need to do concerning any area of your life for He wants to help you. And remember, **"The secret of the Lord is with those who fear Him, and He will show them His covenant." Psalms 25:14**

MINISTERING TO GOD —
A KEY TO A PROSPEROUS LIFE

"Beloved, I pray that you may prosper in all things and be in health, just as your soul prospers." 3 John 2.

"The blessing of the Lord makes one rich, and He adds no sorrow with it." Proverbs 10:22.

It is God's will for us to be prosperous and in good health. God's thoughts toward us are good. He wants us to have good success. **"For I know the thoughts that I think toward you, says the Lord, thoughts of peace and not of evil, to give you a future and a hope." Jeremiah 29:11**

MAN GETS BLESSED FINANCIALLY IN ONE WEEK

On a certain day, as we were in the presence of God, giving unto the Lord glory, honor, and strength, suddenly the Lord gave me a word for a man. The Lord said that within one week He would give him a promotion that would enable him to have more money so He could better his living conditions.

That is exactly what happened to the man. He got a highly paying promotion at his job. A position that paid him good money and very soon he bought most things he had ever desired to have.

The Lord promises us in His Word that as we put Him first and His Kingdom first, and seek after His righteousness, He shall add to us all we need. **"Therefore do not worry, saying, 'What shall we eat?' or 'What shall we drink?' or 'What shall we wear?' for after all these things the gentiles seek. For your heavenly Father knows that you need all these things. But seek first the Kingdom of God and His righteousness, and all these things shall be added to you." Matthew 6:31-33.**

The Lord has many ways how to add these things to us. He knows how to guide and direct our hearts to prosperity. **"Thus says the Lord, our redeemer, the Holy one of Israel: 'I am the Lord your God, who teaches you to profit, who leads you by the way you should go." Isaiah 48:17**

As you minister to the Lord, God will move on your behalf and bring to pass the dream He put in your heart, and you shall walk in it and have good success and God will supply all your needs. **"And my God shall supply all your need according to His riches in glory by Christ Jesus." Philippians 4:19**

I hear the Lord say, *"As you take time to minister to Me,"* says the Lord, *"I will reveal to you what you have to do to increase in substance and I will establish you in all I have promised to you in My Word, says the Lord God Almighty."*

They sing the song
of Moses,
the servant of God,
and
The Song of the Lamb,
saying:
" Great and Marvelous
are Your works,
Lord God Almighty!
Just and true
are your ways,
O King
of the Saints!
Who shall not fear
You, O Lord, and
Glorify Your name?
For You alone are Holy.
For all nations
shall come and worship
before You,
for your judgments
have been manifested."
Revelation 15:3-4

{4}

WORSHIP

A Way of Ministering to God

"A fiery stream issued and came forth from before Him;

ten thousand times ten thousand stood before Him.

The court was seated, and the Books were opened."

Daniel 7:10

Worship of God expressed through singing is part of ministering to God; the only uniqueness about it is that you are making melodies to God. You are musical, and God loves it. True worship by songs is always ascribing glory and honor to God.

Worship in songs is still ministering to God and it is very vital for a congregation of believers, for through worship the church offers spiritual sacrifices to God.

Songs of worship concentrate and have more emphasis on the Lord God the Creator, not just the creation.

Hymns of worship draw you to shower God with the blessings out of gratitude and a thankful heart, which points out God as the answer Himself, as the life Himself, as the only reason that we exist, and He is all we need.

Worship in songs originates from a heart that refuses to emphasize the creation above the Creator. It is intentional. These songs with choice words, birthed through the spirit of a willing vessel, gets us individually and corporately as a church to express our acknowledgement and love to God Himself.

In this kind of atmosphere, people get more conscious of God than themselves and their surroundings. It is one of the highest expressions of faith.

This expression of ministering to God by singing is not governed by our circumstances or what surrounds us. In spite of all, the focus remains on God. Many times in this kind of atmosphere, God reaches out and touches His people with His saving power.

People get healed in their bodies, demons leave people's lives, yokes get broken, burdens get removed, people receive wisdom. They receive direction from the Lord. They receive the Baptism of the Holy Spirit with evidence of speaking in tongues. God does creative miracles.

Churches that have taken worship seriously are not void of the glory of God with tangible manifestations of God's power.

When believers intentionally decide to minister to God

through songs, many times the presence of God fills the place and Jesus touches the people Himself. Most of the time people experience the touch of God within the time of worship! Miracles and wonders take place and the works of the enemy get destroyed.

We are priests. Every born-again believer is a priest and we are a holy priesthood. **"But you are a chosen generation, a royal priesthood, a holy nation, His own special people, that you may proclaim the praises of Him who called you out of darkness into His marvelous light." 1 Peter 2:9**

A priest presents and offers sacrifices to God. In the Old Testament, the expression *"sweet aroma to the Lord"* was used a number of times when priests ministered burnt offerings to the Lord. **"But he shall wash the entrails and the legs with water. Then the priest shall bring it all and burn it on the altar; it is a burnt sacrifice, an offering made by fire, a sweet aroma to the Lord." Leviticus 1:13**

A priest offers something to God. In the New Testament, we do not need to offer burnt sacrifices because Jesus became our sacrificial Lamb on the cross. However, we can offer spiritual sacrifices as we learn who God is and what He has done for us through His Word, then we approach God the way that pleases him. Whenever God accepts our spiritual sacrifices, something to our good from God has to happen.

"**You also, as living stones, are being built up a spiritual house, a holy priesthood, to offer up spiritual sacrifices acceptable to God through Jesus Christ.**" **I Peter 2:5**

Worship is one of the major ways to offer spiritual sacrifices to the Lord.

Building you up through the teaching of the Word is very important, for you learn how to walk in Christ and be a worshipper who is acceptable to God. "**As you therefore have received Christ Jesus the Lord, so walk in Him, rooted and built up in Him and established in the faith, as you have been taught, abounding in it with thanksgiving.**" **Colossians 2:6-7**

We need always to remember that God is holy and we should be holy in our conduct.

"**Therefore, as the elect of God, holy and beloved, put on tender mercies, kindness, humility, meekness, longsuffering, bearing with one another, and forgiving one another, if anyone has a complaint against another; even as Christ forgave you, so you also must do. But above all these things, put on love, which is the bond of perfection. And let the peace of God rule in your hearts to which also you were called in one body; and be thankful. Let the Word of Christ dwell in you richly in all wisdom, teaching and admonishing one another in psalms and hymns and spiritual songs, singing with grace in your hearts** to the Lord. And whatever you do in word or deed, do all in the name of the Lord Jesus, giving thanks to God the Father through Him." **Colossians 3:12-17** Notice the order set up in these scriptures for a life and a church that offers spiritual sacrifices acceptable to God.

First, our walk should be right with God and our conduct needs to be glorifying to God. We need to be people who love others.

Second, we should let the Word of God dwell in us richly. In this way, we know who we are in Christ Jesus, what God says in His Word we can do, and what has been given to us freely by God. "Now we have received, not the spirit of the World, but the Spirit who is from God, that we might know the things that have been freely given to us by God." I Corinthians 2:12 Then we can ask and receive.

Third, we reach out to others by the Word of God and share with them the love of God. We also sing songs of praise to the Lord. These songs minister to us as people of God. Most of the time within these songs there is celebration of victory wrought to us by our Lord Jesus Christ. In praise we celebrate all that God has done for us and what God has given us, as well as what we are in Him.

Fourth, now we are in good shape to offer worship to God. That is to sing with grace in our hearts to the Lord. We do all this in the name of our Lord Jesus Christ.

Fifth, the Lord reaches out to us, touches our lives, blesses our bread and water and takes sickness out of our midst. **"So you shall serve the Lord your God, and He will bless your bread and your water, and I will take sickness away from the midst of you."** Exodus 23:25

As the glory of God fills our lives and our services, and miracles, signs wonders take place, plus God, speaking to us by Word of Wisdom, Word of Knowledge, prophecy, tongues and interpretation, the next automatic thing is spontaneous thanksgiving.

Any church or body of believers anywhere on earth can experience and live filled with God's power, miracles, wonders and signs. God is not a respecter of persons. **"Then Peter opened his mouth and said: 'In truth, I perceive that God shows no partiality. But in every nation whoever fears Him and works righteousness is accepted by Him.'"** Acts 10:34-35

In our worship services at Kamwokya, Kampala City, Uganda, we saw God touching and healing people every day. They got healed from cancer, tumors, headaches, abdominal problems, heart diseases, AIDS, kidney problems, and many other infirmities.

People received houses, jobs, cars, money, and scholarships to go to universities, from the Lord. People got born again every day and filled with the Holy Spirit with evidence of speaking in tongues. Sometimes the whole place could get so electrified by the presence of God that everyone felt Him. I didn't need to tell them that the Lord was in our midst for they felt Him for themselves.

People's lives were filled with joy and gladness; it was a time of refreshment from the Lord. Demons could not stay hidden in any of God's people. The demons left screaming, tormented by the power of God. Ministries got birthed in people's lives.

People loved attending church every day for God Himself energized them. When they went out after the services, signs and wonders followed them. God used them as well as worked with them.

If God could use even handkerchiefs and aprons to heal the sick, He can use you. **"Now God worked unusual miracles by the hands of Paul, so that even handkerchiefs or aprons were brought from his body to the sick, and the diseases left them and the evil spirits went out of them." Acts 19:11-12**

I have seen this happen. We have prayed over handkerchiefs in the name of Jesus and when placed on the sick, the diseases left them.

Beloved, this is what this book is partly for. It is time for great exploits; it is time to take nations for Jesus, time to take cities for Jesus. It is time to go forth with God's power in our lives and help people. The time for us to bear much fruit for the Kingdom of God is now.

Every church that confesses Jesus Christ as Lord and Savior should be able to move in the glory of God and should be inhabited by the tangible presence of God. We should be able to operate in the priestly anointing through ministering to God. We should not be rejected because of lack of knowledge. **"My people are destroyed for lack of knowledge. Because you have rejected knowledge, I also will reject you from being priest for Me; because you have forgotten the law of your God, I also will forget your children." Hosea 4:6**

Let us embrace the revealed knowledge of God to us. Let us be a people moving by the Spirit of God, a people of power.

Let us glorify God in the land so that many may come to the Lord, for these are the latter days.

"Now it shall come to pass in the latter days that the mountain of the Lord's house shall be established on the top of the mountains and shall be exalted above the hills and all nations shall flow to it; Many people shall come and say, 'Come, and let us go up to the mountain of the Lord to the House of the God of Jacob. He will teach us His ways and we shall walk in His paths.'" Isaiah 2:2

"LIKEWISE THE SPIRIT
ALSO HELPS IN OUR
WEAKNESSES.
FOR WE DO NOT KNOW
WHAT WE SHOULD
PRAY FOR AS WE OUGHT,
BUT THE SPIRIT
HIMSELF MAKES
INTERCESSION FOR US
WITH
GROANINGS WHICH
CANNOT BE UTTERED.
HE WHO SEARCHES
THE HEARTS KNOWS
WHAT THE MIND OF
THE SPIRIT IS,
BECAUSE
HE MAKES INTERCESSION
FOR THE SAINTS
ACCORDING TO THE WILL
OF GOD."
ROMANS 8:26-27

{5}

MINISTERING TO GOD

Through Speaking in Tongues

**"For they heard them speak with
tongues and magnify God." Acts 10:46**

We are living at a very important time of Bible prophecy.
We are living at the time when we expect the coming of our Lord
Jesus Christ for His bride — the Church. Changes are taking
place around the nations. The World is starting to adopt a global
vision in an effort to solve challenges that they have perceived
to be a threat to all humans.

The thinking of the people is changing. People are realizing that though they are living in different nations, they all dwell on the same earth. They breathe the same air and are all facing the same grave challenges, many of which are a threat to human existence such as earthquakes, deadly plagues, wars, moral deterioration, demonic occurrences, rumors of war, terrorist activities, etc. **"And you will hear of wars and rumors of wars. See that you are not troubled; for all these things must come to pass, but the end is not yet. For nation will rise against nation, and Kingdom against Kingdom. And there will be famines, pestilences, and earthquakes in various places. All these are the beginning of sorrows...And this Gospel of the Kingdom will be preached in all the world as a witness to all the nations, and then the end will come." Matthew 24:6-14**

You notice that Jesus had a global vision already, though physically He was preaching, teaching and healing people in Israel and the surrounding area.

In His sermons, He always addressed all the world and expressed God's love for the World. **"For God so loved the World that He gave His only begotten Son, that whoever believes in Him should not perish but have everlasting life." John 3:16**

Jesus had all people in mind, all nations in mind. He had Uganda in East Africa in mind. He had Israel in the Middle East in mind. He had United States of America on the American continent in mind. He had Australia in mind. He had Mexico in mind. He had Nigeria in Northwest Africa in mind, plus Britain, Canada, Saudi Arabia, India, ……. and so on.

The vision of the body of Christ is global and we all are one another's keeper. All of us are supposed to be watchmen for one another. We can't live with the Cain's attitude. **"Then the Lord said to Cain, 'where is Abel your brother?' He said, 'I do not know. Am I my brother's keeper?'" Genesis 4:9**

We need to have, as well as be, everything the Lord God says. We are not just prospering for ourselves. God gives us so much that we may be able to pass some to His people.

"Therefore, putting away lying, let each one of you speak truth with his neighbor, for we are members of one another." Ephesians 4:25.

"Let him who stole steal no longer, but rather let him labor, working with his hands what is good, that he may have something to give him who has need." Ephesians 4:28.

The Lord not only has provided healing for you —
"Who Himself bore our sins in His own body on the tree, that we, having died to sins, might live for righteousness - by whose stripes you were healed." 1 Peter2:24 -- but also wants to heal the sick through your life. **"And these signs will follow those who believe: in my name they will cast out demons; they will speak with new tongues; they will take up serpents, and if they drink anything deadly, it will by no means hurt them, they will lay hand on the sick, and they will recover." Mark 16:17-18.**

Everything said in Mark 16:17-18, by our Lord Jesus Christ, the Lord of the church, the Great Shepherd, the way, the truth, and the life and no one comes to the Father except through Him is supposed to be a part of the believer's life and the church as the body of Christ. **"Jesus said to him, 'I am the way, the truth, and the life. No one comes to the Father except through me.'" John 14:6**

In Mark 16:17, the Lord is talking about those who believe those who have received Jesus Christ as their personal Savior and Lord. **"For there is no distinction between Jew and Greek, for the same Lord over all is rich to all who call upon Him. For whoever calls on the name of the Lord shall be saved." Romans 10:12**

Six things you need to recognize in Mark 16:17 about a believer.

1. Casting out demons in the name of Jesus: "**...But Paul, greatly annoyed, turned and said to the spirit, 'I command you in the name of Jesus Christ to come out of her' and he came out that very hour.**" **Acts 16:18** Paul was a believer.

2. Speaking with other tongues: "**And they were all filled with the Holy Spirit and began to speak with other tongues, as the Spirit gave them utterance.**"

Acts 2:4 All of those people were believers.

3. Serpents rendered powerless through the power of God: "**...But when Paul had gathered a bundle of sticks and laid them on the fire, a viper came out because of the heat, and fastened on his hand. So when the natives saw the creature hanging from his hand, they said to one another, 'No doubt this man is a murderer, whom though he has escaped the sea, yet justice does not allow to live.' But he shook off the creature into the fire and suffered no harm. However, they were expecting that he would swell up or suddenly fall down dead. But after they had looked for a long time and saw no harm come to him, they changed their minds and said that he was a god.**" **Acts 28:3-6**

4. Deadly drinks are rendered harmless through the power of God: **"Then the men of the city said to Elisha, 'Please notice, the situation of this city is pleasant, as my Lord sees, but the water is bad, and the ground is barren.' And He said, 'Bring me a new bowl, and put salt in it' So they brought it to Him. Then He went out to the source of the water, and cast in the salt there and said, 'Thus says the Lord: "I have healed this water; from it there shall be no more death or barrenness."' So the water remains healed to this day, according to the word of Elisha, which he spoke." II Kings 2:19-22**

God is able to destroy poison's power to harm the believer.

5. They will lay hands on the sick and they will

recover: **"And Ananias went his way and entered the house; and laying his hands on him he said, 'Brother Saul, the Lord Jesus, who appeared to you on the road as you came, has sent me that you may receive you sight and be filled with the Holy Spirit.'**

Immediately there fell from his eyes something like scales, and he received his sight at once, and he arose and was baptized" Acts 9:17-18 Ananias was a believer. "Now there was a certain disciple at Damascus named Ananias; and to him the Lord said in a vision, 'Ananaias,' and he said, 'Here I am Lord.'" Acts 9:10

6. These signs will follow those who believe: "Then Peter said to them, 'Repent, and let every one of you be baptized in the name of Jesus Chris for the remission of sins; and you shall receive the gift of the Holy Spirit. For the promise is to you and to your children, and to all who are afar off, as many as the Lord our God will call." Acts 2:38-39 Anyone can become a believer and God is not willing that any should perish. "The Lord is not slack concerning His promise, as some count slackness, but is longsuffering toward us, not willing that any should perish but that all should come to repentance." II Peter 3:9

And if you have not yet given your life to Jesus Christ and received Him as your personal Savior, just go ahead and do it right now. Say these words. Repeat after me: *"Lord God, I do believe that you raised the Lord Jesus Christ from the dead, and Lord Jesus, I do receive you into my heart as my Lord and Savior today and I confess with my mouth that You are the Lord and my Savior."*

"That if you confess with your mouth the Lord Jesus and believe in your heart that God has raised Him from the dead, you will be saved." Romans 10:9

I have written that prayer because the Lord spoke to me that this book is going to be read by millions of people and many of them will get born again and become believers.

Remember, we are dealing with Tongues as a way of ministering to God, a key to a prosperous life and church filled with God's power, miracles, signs, and wonders.

According to Mark 15:17, every believer can receive the baptism of the Holy Spirit with evidence of speaking in tongues for Jesus has made it clear that these signs follow those who believe.

You are a believer. You can receive the baptism of the Holy Spirit with evidence of speaking in tongues.

Jesus Christ baptizes people with the Holy Spirit and fire. John the Baptist testified to this in Matthew 3:11 "**I indeed baptize you with water unto repentance, but He who is coming after me is mightier than I, whose sandals I am not worth to carry. He will baptize you with the Holy Spirit and fire.**" John the Baptist was talking about Jesus Christ the son of the Living God.

In the Gospel of Mark, we have John the Baptist testifying about the same again. "**And He preached saying, 'There comes one after me who is mightier than I, whose sandal strap I am not worthy to stoop down and loose. I indeed baptized you with water, but He will baptize you with the Holy Spirit.'**" **Mark 1:7-8**

The Baptism of the Holy Spirit is different from the baptism in water, in the Book of Acts, the 10th Chapter, the people to whom Peter was preaching got baptized in the Holy Spirit before they were baptized in water. "**While Peter was still speaking these words, the Holy Spirit fell upon all those who heard the Word. And those of the circumcision who believed were astonished, as many as came with Peter, because the gift of the Holy Spirit had been poured out on the Gentiles also. For they heard them speak with tongues and magnify God.**" **Acts 10:44-46**

I know I am dealing with a very sensitive area in the body of Christ, for there are many believers who are yet to receive the Baptism of the Holy Spirit with evidence of speaking with other tongues that is very crucial in ministering to God. An experience can change around your life and bring you to a place of great power, wisdom, signs, miracles and wonderful experiences with the Lord God Almighty.

How I received the Baptism of the Holy Spirit

Being someone from the Catholic Church background, when I received the Baptism in the Holy Spirit in 1985, in Hong Kong, China, everything in me changed for the better. All the time I served as an altar boy in the Catholic Church, at Saint Peter's Cathedral, Sambya, Kampala City, Uganda, I never saw anybody speaking in tongues and I never had any priest invite us for the Baptism of the Holy Spirit with evidence of speaking in tongues. Since we never had Bibles to read ourselves, and my teachers at St. Peter's Primary School didn't mention anything about it, I didn't know about this heavenly gift. Possibly, if I had someone to show me the scriptures and help me to understand it, I would have received the baptism of the Holy Spirit earlier.

"So Philip ran to him and heard him reading the prophet Isaiah, and said, 'Do you understand what you are reading?' and he said, 'How can I, unless someone guides me?' and he asked Philip to come up and sit with Him." Acts 8:30-31 Philip, the evangelist, helped this man, who loved to worship the Lord God, to understand the Scriptures.

This is the purpose of this book. God has sent me to you to help you understand as well as get you to receive what was provided for you two thousand years ago. It is only awaiting you to come to God and receive, for you love to worship God. You love to give unto God glory, honor and power due to Him. You have been feeling deep inside you there is more you can do to magnify God, but you need divine help from God, Himself.

You say to God, lovingly, all you know to say and you reach a time when you run out of words. Still, because of your desire to love Him and shower Him with your love, you are searching in your hearts for words and what to do. The answer is right here! Only keep on this journey with me. We shall get there.

I joined Saint Henry's College, in Kitovu, in Masaka, Uganda, where I spent six years studying. I did the ordinary level and advanced level in this very highly esteemed college in Africa. Every day we went to church. We attended the Catholic Chapel at the College.

After some time, it was left to the students to decide whether to attend Mass every day early in the morning or in the evening, before prep. But for the first year, we all had to attend church services every morning. Because I loved God, I decided to attend Mass every single day I was at college. Still I never saw anybody speaking in tongues and I never had anyone invite us to the Baptism of the Holy Spirit. Nor did I ever see any priest or brother cast out demons from the students, though it was obvious, the way some students were mean to others, there must have been some devils in them!

I never saw the preachers lay hands on anyone to receive healing. We had to only depend on the College Clinic or the hospitals in the area to look to for help. Some people, facing tough spiritual challenges, had to look to psychics, astrologers, or witch doctors for help. Many of us never knew that someone could get born again for it was never taught. **"My people are destroyed for lack of knowledge…." Hosea 4:6**

Remember, this was a college with instructors in all subjects: Luganda, history, chemistry, geography, fine arts, technical drawing, English literature, physics, mathematics, economics, accounting, French, biology, religious education, music, and typing.

Our tutor in Religious Education could not explain the Bible to us as an anointed man of God would. He only presented the Bible to us as a great historical book and a book of great moral virtue that could help us to be students of good conduct. That is how I received it, though most of the time I had the highest marks in the Religious Education Exams, with straight A's. The presentation could not get us anywhere in God, spiritually.

One of our instructors was a Catholic priest from Ireland. This man was teaching us pure mathematics at the advanced level. By this time, I was doing pure mathematics, applied mathematics, chemistry, physics and general paper. I was getting ready to join the university for Engineering.

This man was our class master and he really loved to see us succeed in our studies. The fact that he was a priest as well, he made sure that every time before he started lecturing we stood up and prayed the Lord's Prayer. He even encouraged us to attend mass every day at the school chapel.

Mind you, half the students in our class were not Catholics, but he always invited all of us. However, we never heard him mention anything about the importance of the baptism of the Holy Spirit.

I joined Makerere University in 1981. I got born again in Lumumba Hall that year. My fellow students, who knew about salvation led me to the Lord. After some time, I got another government scholarship to go to a university of my choice in China in a field of any kind of Engineering I wanted. I chose irrigation and water conservation engineering, for my Father owned a ranch of five square miles in Uganda. I felt that I could be helpful to make it very productive, as I would also be working for the government.

While I was at Hahai University in Nanjing, China, I met an American professor who was teaching in the medical school at Nanjing University of Medicine. This man loved God and one day he loaned me a book with a title "The Holy Spirit."

You could sense the presence of God through the pages of that book. I read that book five times, and I concluded, without doubt, that I needed the baptism of the Holy Spirit with the evidence of speaking with other tongues.

I want you to know the kind of person I was then; I was a scientist used to proving everything mathematically and scientifically. Even at that time of school, at the university it was a time of much studying, proving things and advancing in knowledge. The book fitted my lifestyle. The author simply and clearly, by the Holy Spirit of God, explained with Scriptures the importance of having the Baptism of the Holy Spirit. I started asking God to baptize me with the Holy

Spirit with evidence of speaking in tongues. Surely, our Lord Jesus Christ could baptize me in the Holy Spirit. **"If you then, being evil, know how to give good gifts to your children, how much more will your heavenly Father give the Holy Spirit to those who ask Him!" Luke 11:13** I would come before God every day with hands raised up, expecting Him to baptize me with the Holy Spirit with the evidence of speaking a heavenly language. I wanted that fountain of heavenly language to start flowing through my life. **"Jesus answered and said to her, 'Whoever drinks of this water will thirst again, but whoever drinks of the water that I shall give him will never thirst. But the water I give him will become a fountain of water springing up into everlasting life.'" John 4:13-14** I expectantly wanted this fountain of the Holy Spirit to become a reality in my life. I wanted, expectantly, to receive. I went to this man who had loaned me the book and asked him what I should do. I needed the baptism of Holy Spirit so desperately. I knew I would get into a higher level of operation in everything to do with my life for the Holy Spirit is a helper. **"But the helper, the Holy Spirit, whom the Father will send in My name, He will teach you all things, and bring to your remembrance all things that I said to you." John 14:26**

Jesus also said, **"If you love Me, keep My commandments. And I will pray the Father, and He will give you another Helper, that He may abide with you forever, the Spirit of truth, whom the World cannot receive, because it neither sees Him nor knows Him, but you know Him, for He dwells with you and He will be in you. I will not leave you orphans; I will come to you." John 14:15-18**

I was determined to do anything it took to receive the baptism of the Holy Spirit. Remember, at the university most of the students, especially the Chinese students, had been taught that there was no God.

And the foreign students from other countries, none of them knew what it was to be baptized in the Holy Spirit with evidence of speaking in tongues. Most of them were just religious. They were just going through ceremonies as their religions taught them. They didn't know that a person could be filled with the Holy Spirit.

"Therefore do not be unwise, but understand what the will of the Lord is. And do not be drunk with wine, in which is dissipation; but be filled with the Spirit, speaking to one another in psalms and hymns and spiritual songs, singing and making melody in your hearts to the Lord." Ephesians 5:17-19 So, I couldn't find help from the people I was among, as they didn't know.

The professor who loaned me the book advised me to go to Hong Kong during the holiday and visit with the New Covenant Church over there because that church was very prosperous in God. It was alive in the word of God. They took all the help the Holy Spirit could give them.

They had embraced the doctrine of the baptism of the Holy Spirit and they spoke in tongues as the Holy Spirit gave them utterance. They were full of joy and strong in our Lord Jesus Christ. I decided to go there.

It was a Sunday evening when I arrived at the Church. The preacher was teaching about the Holy Spirit! This man was an apostle by call and he went around the world strengthening churches. He had flown in that morning from another continent and was to leave that day.

Understand, apostles do exist today. **"And He, Himself, gave some to be apostles, some prophets, some evangelists, and some pastors and teachers, for the equipping of the saints for the work of ministry, for the edifying of the Body of Christ." Ephesians 4:11-12**

No wonder this church was very effective in Hong Kong, China. The atmosphere during their worship was charged with the presence of God. There was expectation for the Lord to touch His people and heal them. To this body of believers, God was omnipotent, not just by speech but by manifested acts of God in their midst.

The pastor of the church had an understanding of the need of the office of an apostle, a prophet, evangelists, teachers, for the equipping of the saints for the work of ministry.

That was my first time to attend such a lively service. The man of God that preached that day was constantly reaching out to us from the Bible.

As I sat there listening to the ministry of the Word, I started sensing a holy presence of God around me, my lips were stuttering like they were about to say something. Deep in my Spirit I knew I was receiving the baptism of the Holy Spirit.

After the service, I approached the pastor of the church and told him that I wanted to receive the baptism of the Holy Spirit with evidence of speaking in tongues. He responded eagerly by taking me to the apostle who preached that day.

This man of God and six other men of God knelt down with me and held up my hands as they asked Jesus to baptize me with the Holy Spirit. What happened next surpassed all the science I had learned. Don't forget, this is happening to a student of engineering at a university who knew most things mathematically and scientifically.

During that prayer, I felt the glory of God intensifying all around me. It was like I was caught up in a powerfully, invisible, glistening presence. It was as if the whole place was electrified. This powerful glory filled my body. It was like my entire being was placed in a very high voltage electrical current, but this power was not destructive.

I felt like every cell of my being was being energized. Another phenomenon took place. Suddenly I felt like there was a great rock around me. My hands remained upward, held up by this great rock. It was so real, though I couldn't see this strong presence of God like a rock around me, it was very real. **"But the Lord has been my defense, and my God the rock of my refuge." Psalms 94:22**

Suddenly words started coming forth out of my Spirit in my belly and I started speaking in tongues. This went on for something like twenty minutes. I remember I cried like a baby for the joy; then I laughed like a child. I also spoke with tongues and interpretation for about thirty minutes. That is one of the areas that amazed me. I operated in the gift of tongues and interpretation. **"To another the working of miracles, to another prophecy, to another discerning of spirits, to another different kinds of tongues, to another the interpretation of tongues. But one and the same spirit works all these things, distributing to each one and individually as He wills." I Corinthians 12:10-11**

God dealt with me in a way that surpassed all my natural logic. My mouth was speaking in tongues and interpretation without me controlling it. It was such a beautiful experience! I could hear what was being said to me through my mouth. I was completely alert and I knew this was a miracle and a sign to me. God spoke to me by my mouth, about my life, all the way from birth to that day.

He also spoke to me about my future. He pointed out His purpose for my life and the call of God on me. Some of what He said to me that day was that, *"You shall put the deepest truth into words by revelational knowledge"* and *"I will do things in your life you have never imagined or thought."* All these I have seen.

I have seen God touching people's lives as I minister in the church services, as well as crusades, and also when I am praying with people individually in ways that amazed me.

This book you are reading today is a result of the Holy Spirit guiding me by revelation knowledge, based on the Holy Scriptures. **"Then Jesus said to those Jews who believed Him, 'If you abide in My Word, you are My disciples indeed and you shall know the truth, and the truth shall make you free.'" John 8:32.**

The gift of tongues and interpretation is still operational in my life. Many times the Lord gives me a word for His church during services and a Word in tongues and interpretation for individuals as well. Something else the Lord has enabled me to realize is that sometimes the tongues spoken by people are just ministering to God, magnifying the Lord God Almighty, tongues that are worshipping God. **"For they heard them speak with tongues and magnify God." Acts 10:46**

You may not have the same experiences as I had when I received the baptism of the Holy Spirit. Still, you will be receiving the same Holy Spirit as every other believer received with evidence of speaking in tongues.

Another thing I have observed is there are a number of times in worship services, or services where people have gathered to give unto God glory, honor and power due to Him, that suddenly the Lord just goes ahead and baptizes them with the Holy Spirit.

They suddenly start singing or speaking in a heavenly language that brings a fundamental change and helps in their passion to minister to God.

You don't have to wait or tarry for long to receive the baptism of the Holy Spirit. You only need to be willing and obedient. Those people in Acts 10 received the baptism of the

Holy Spirit the same day they believed. I have seen this happen again and again.

A Moslem Woman Receives the Baptism of the Holy Spirit

A Moslem person came to our church services on a Thursday evening, and while I was teaching at the pulpit, the Lord gave me a Word of Knowledge. I just knew, and I spoke it forth. **"For to one is given the Word of Wisdom through the Spirit, to another the Word of Knowledge through the same Spirit."** 1 Corinthians 12:8

The Word was someone was going through a legal court challenge and the Lord was going to help that person.

When this woman heard what I said by the Spirit of God, she raised her hand, astonished. This was her first time to attend a Christian Church service. I called her to come forth. The Lord was already touching her as she came to the front.

The moment I said the Lord is changing the matter around for her, the glory of the Lord was so strong on her that she couldn't stand in it. **"And when I saw Him, I fell at His feet as dead. But He laid His right hand on me, saying to me 'Do not be afraid; I am the First and the Last.'"** Revelation 1:17

Later, when she stood up, she told us she was a Moslem and one of her neighbors, a believer in our Lord Jesus Christ, brought her to church that day.

Two things amazed her: that God had revealed her situation to me without her telling me, the other thing was that she felt a strong presence of God and God touched her even though she was not a Christian yet.

She didn't get born again that day. After one week she came back testifying that the Lord God, in the name of Jesus Christ, had delivered her from the legal problem and she wanted to get born again — to become a Christian!

When I led her through the prayer of salvation, the Lord baptized her with the Holy Spirit with evidence of speaking in other tongues. This woman became a great intercessor in the church, a person who knows how to wait on the Lord.

It is very important you to take some time and search the Scriptures by yourself so you can receive, as well as help others to receive. It is not right for someone to be unfair- minded and reject the counsel of God. It is good to search the Scriptures like the people of Berea in **Acts 17: "Then the brethren immediately sent Paul and Silas away by night to Berea. When they arrived, they went into the synagogue of the Jews. These were more fair-minded than those in**

Thessalonica in that they received the Word with all readiness, and searched the Scriptures daily to find out whether these things were so. Therefore many of them believed, and also not a few of the Greeks, prominent women as well as men." Acts 17:10-12

The Gift of the Holy Spirit is for all believers. When you ask God to baptize you with the Holy Spirit in the name of Jesus, that is exactly what our Lord Jesus Christ will do for you.

Three points to note — Baptism of the Holy Spirit with evidence of speaking in Tongues:

1. God is omniscient. **"For in Him we live and move and have our being...." Acts 17:28** God is very near to us and also is at all other places we are not. **"Am I a God near at hand; says the Lord, And not a God afar off?" Jeremiah 23:23**

2. God is all-powerfully omnipotent. **"When Abram was ninety-nine years old, the Lord appeared to Abram and said to him, 'I am Almighty God; Walk before me and be blameless.'" Genesis 17:1** Nothing can withstand His mightiness.

3. Your responsibility is to ask. God is able to get you to receive the baptism of the Holy Spirit with evidence of speaking in tongues in the name of Jesus, but you have to ask. **"If a son asks for bread from any father among you, will He give Him a stone? Or if he asks for a fish, will he give him a serpent instead of a fish? Or if he asks for an egg, will he offer him a scorpion? If you then, being evil, know how to give good gifts to your children, how much more will your heavenly Father give the Holy Spirit to those who ask Him?" Luke 11:11-13**

It is very important when you note those three points that you may not be nervous about the receiving of the Baptism of the Holy Spirit with evidence of speaking in tongues.

God cannot allow the devils to get in you when you ask for His Spirit. In fact, what will happen is that the devils in you, if there are any, will have to leave your life as the Holy Spirit fills your being and gives you a heavenly language.

I have preached around the world. I have preached in China, America, Africa. I have found out that people basically, when it comes to things of God, all undergo the same challenges. All are battling with the same old religious spirits.

Religious spirits are very tricky, for they have a form of godliness but deny what it takes to function in God's power.

"...having a form of godliness, but denying its power. And from such people turn away!" II Timothy 3:1-5

If there has ever been a time when we needed all that God says we should have in our churches and our lives, it is now.

A church of believers filled with the Holy Spirit with evidence of speaking in tongues is very vital. That church can accomplish a lot. The tangible power of God is among them.

Those people can corporately minister to God with the help of the Holy Spirit who gives them utterance. No wonder as they do that on purpose, the gifts of the Holy Spirit flourish easily in that environment. Then God gives direction, heals His people, and deposits information in His people's lives that enables them to deal with everyday challenges.

When you speak in tongues, you speak mysteries, far placed beauty to God, by the Holy Spirit. **"For he who speaks in a tongue does not speak to men but to God, for no one understands him; however, in the Spirit he speaks mysteries." I Corinthians 14:2** In Acts 2 the Lord allowed the people, in the hearing of the disciples who had just been filled with the Holy Spirit and were speaking in other tongues as the Holy Spirit gave them utterance, to understand the mysteries they uttered out through their mouths, for each heard in their language.

"**Cretans and Arabs, we hear them speaking in our own tongues the wonderful works of God."** Acts 2:11

God is seeking true worshippers. **"But the hour is coming, and now is when the true worshippers will worship the father in spirit and truth; for the father is seeking such to worship him."** John 4:23

Ministering to God through speaking in tongues brings about a prosperous life/church filled with God's power, miracles, signs and wonders.

People are looking for answers, about how to live, how to raise their children. They are in need of physical healing, plus emotional healing; they need money to take care of their day-to-day obligations. They want a touch from God, many are worn out by religions, and they are tired of ceremonies.

They need a real thing, not fables and stories; they need to know how to overcome the wicked one. Their only hope is you to come to them in the power of God, through our Lord Jesus Christ and get them helped. That is why a church or a believer should not be void of the power of God. And the power of God comes when we are in His presence ministering to Him. Amen!

Please be a partner to this ministry by sowing your seed in this good ground that we may get this message to as many people as possible.

Honor the lord with your possessions and with the first fruits of all your increase; so your barns will be filled with plenty, and your vats will overflow with new wine. Proverbs 3: 9-10

Many have done that and
God has healed them miraculously!

Leonard Kayiwa Ministries
P.O. Box 1898
Bolingbrook, Illinois 60440
(224) 440-6992

kayiwaministries@yahoo.com

Other Books by the Author

1. What Happens When We Pray And Believe God

2. Receive Your Healing in The Name of Jesus
   Christ of Nazareth

3. You Can Prosper In God

Order by writing to:
Kayiwa Ministries
P.O. Box 1898
Bolingbrook, IL 60440

You can also can order book through our websites:

www.kayiwaministries.org

www.ministeringtogod.com

www.leonardkayiwa.com

email: Kayiwaministries@yahoo.com

telephone: 224-440-6692

World Evangelism Healing Worship Center International Inc.

The Isaiah 58 Blessing:

You can also receive a copy of this book for a donation of $20.00 or more in support of the drive to help orphans.

Bishop Leonard MP Kayiwa founded a 501(c)3 tax exempt church organization for helping orphans in different countries in Africa.

This organization, registered in U.S.A. and Africa, is called **AFRICAN CHILDREN BENEVOLENCE FOUNDATION INTERNATIONAL, INC.**

We shall send you a tax-deductible receipt for your gift towards helping God's children, the orphans.

We will also send you a copy of this beautiful book. Make your check payable to:
A.C.B.F.I.,Inc. or African Children Benevolence Foundation International, Inc. P.O. Box 1898 Bolingbrook, IL 60440

Visit ACBFI websites:
www.acbfi.org

find video clip on:
www.kayiwaministries.org
www.ministeringtogod.com

You can also send your gift online. Thank you.